# 50 Morning Meals Made Memorable
## Recipes for Home

By: Kelly Johnson

# Table of Contents

- Classic Buttermilk Pancakes
- Avocado Toast with Poached Egg
- French Toast with Maple Syrup
- Blueberry Muffins
- Breakfast Burrito with Sausage and Eggs
- Greek Yogurt Parfait with Fresh Berries
- Scrambled Eggs with Smoked Salmon
- Cinnamon Rolls with Cream Cheese Frosting
- Veggie Omelette
- Banana Pancakes with Nutella
- Chia Seed Pudding with Almond Milk
- Breakfast Quesadilla with Cheese and Bacon
- Sourdough Toast with Avocado and Tomato
- Belgian Waffles with Strawberries and Whipped Cream
- Breakfast Hash with Potatoes and Chorizo
- Spinach and Feta Quiche
- Oatmeal with Caramelized Bananas
- Bagel with Lox and Cream Cheese
- Breakfast Tacos with Chorizo and Egg
- Lemon Ricotta Pancakes
- Shakshuka (Eggs Poached in Spicy Tomato Sauce)
- Breakfast Sandwich with Ham and Cheese
- Peanut Butter and Jelly Waffles
- Huevos Rancheros
- Biscuits and Gravy
- Smoked Salmon Bagel with Cream Cheese
- Apple Cinnamon French Toast Bake
- Breakfast Pizza with Eggs and Bacon
- Overnight Oats with Berries and Honey
- Sausage and Egg Breakfast Casserole
- Strawberry Banana Smoothie Bowl
- Corned Beef Hash with Fried Eggs
- Breakfast Croissant with Ham and Swiss
- Pumpkin Pancakes with Whipped Cream
- Breakfast Enchiladas with Salsa Verde
- Blueberry Scones

- Quinoa Breakfast Bowl with Spinach and Egg
- Cinnamon Sugar Donuts
- Breakfast BLT (Bacon, Lettuce, Tomato) Sandwich
- Breakfast Bread Pudding with Berries
- Sweet Potato Hash with Poached Eggs
- Cranberry Orange Muffins
- Breakfast Strata with Ham and Cheese
- Nutella Stuffed French Toast
- Breakfast Crepes with Fresh Fruit
- Bacon and Cheese Breakfast Pizza
- English Breakfast (Eggs, Bacon, Sausage, Beans)
- Lemon Poppy Seed Pancakes
- Breakfast Biscuit Sandwich with Egg and Sausage
- Yogurt and Berry Smoothie

**Classic Buttermilk Pancakes**

**Ingredients:**

- 1 cup all-purpose flour
- 1 tablespoon sugar
- 1 teaspoon baking powder
- 1/2 teaspoon baking soda
- 1/4 teaspoon salt
- 1 cup buttermilk
- 1 large egg
- 2 tablespoons unsalted butter, melted
- Butter or oil for cooking

**Instructions:**

1. **Preheat Griddle or Pan:** Heat a griddle or non-stick skillet over medium heat. You want it to be hot enough to cook the pancakes evenly.
2. **Mix Dry Ingredients:** In a mixing bowl, whisk together the flour, sugar, baking powder, baking soda, and salt.
3. **Mix Wet Ingredients:** In another bowl, whisk together the buttermilk, egg, and melted butter until well combined.
4. **Combine:** Pour the wet ingredients into the dry ingredients and stir gently until just combined. It's okay if there are a few lumps in the batter.
5. **Cook Pancakes:** Add a small amount of butter or oil to the hot griddle or skillet. Ladle about 1/4 cup of batter onto the griddle for each pancake. Cook until bubbles form on the surface of the pancake and the edges look set, about 2-3 minutes.
6. **Flip:** Carefully flip the pancakes with a spatula and cook until golden brown on the other side, about 1-2 minutes more.
7. **Serve:** Transfer the pancakes to a plate and serve warm with your favorite toppings such as maple syrup, fresh berries, or whipped cream.
8. **Enjoy:** Repeat with the remaining batter, adding more butter or oil to the griddle as needed. Serve the pancakes hot and enjoy!

**Tips:**

- To keep pancakes warm while cooking in batches, place them on a baking sheet in a 200°F (93°C) oven until ready to serve.
- If you don't have buttermilk, you can make a substitute by adding 1 tablespoon of lemon juice or vinegar to 1 cup of milk. Let it sit for 5-10 minutes until it curdles slightly before using.
- Avoid overmixing the pancake batter to keep the pancakes fluffy and tender.

**Avocado Toast with Poached Egg**

**Ingredients:**

- 1 ripe avocado
- 2 slices of your favorite bread (such as whole grain or sourdough)
- 2 eggs
- Salt and pepper, to taste
- Red pepper flakes (optional, for garnish)
- Fresh herbs (such as cilantro or parsley), chopped (optional for garnish)

**Instructions:**

1. **Prepare the Avocado:**
   - Cut the avocado in half lengthwise. Remove the pit and scoop the flesh into a bowl. Use a fork to mash the avocado until it reaches your desired consistency (smooth or slightly chunky). Season with salt and pepper to taste.
2. **Toast the Bread:**
   - Toast the slices of bread until they are golden brown and crispy.
3. **Poach the Eggs:**
   - Fill a medium-sized pot with water and bring it to a gentle simmer (not boiling). Add a splash of vinegar (optional, helps the egg whites to set faster).
   - Crack one egg into a small bowl or cup. Using a spoon, create a gentle whirlpool in the simmering water. Carefully pour the egg into the center of the whirlpool. Repeat with the second egg.
   - Cook the eggs for about 3-4 minutes until the whites are set but the yolks are still runny. Use a slotted spoon to carefully remove each poached egg from the water and place them on a paper towel to drain excess water.
4. **Assemble the Avocado Toast:**
   - Spread a generous amount of mashed avocado onto each slice of toasted bread.
5. **Top with Poached Eggs:**
   - Carefully place one poached egg on each slice of avocado toast.
6. **Season and Garnish:**
   - Sprinkle with a pinch of salt, pepper, and red pepper flakes (if using). Add chopped fresh herbs for extra flavor and color.
7. **Serve Immediately:**
   - Enjoy your avocado toast with poached egg while it's still warm and the yolk is deliciously runny!

This recipe is versatile, so feel free to customize it with additional toppings such as cherry tomatoes, feta cheese, or a drizzle of balsamic glaze. It's a satisfying and wholesome breakfast that's quick to make and full of healthy fats and protein.

## French Toast with Maple Syrup

### Ingredients:

- 4 slices of bread (thick slices like brioche or Texas toast work well)
- 2 large eggs
- 1/2 cup milk
- 1 teaspoon vanilla extract
- 1/2 teaspoon ground cinnamon
- Pinch of salt
- Butter or oil, for cooking
- Maple syrup, for serving
- Fresh berries, powdered sugar, or whipped cream (optional, for garnish)

### Instructions:

1. **Prepare the French Toast Batter:**
   - In a shallow bowl or baking dish, whisk together the eggs, milk, vanilla extract, cinnamon, and a pinch of salt until well combined.
2. **Soak the Bread:**
   - Heat a non-stick skillet or griddle over medium heat and add a small amount of butter or oil to coat the surface.
   - Dip each slice of bread into the egg mixture, allowing it to soak for about 20-30 seconds on each side. Make sure the bread is well coated but not soggy.
3. **Cook the French Toast:**
   - Place the soaked bread slices onto the heated skillet or griddle. Cook for 2-3 minutes on each side, or until golden brown and cooked through. Adjust the heat if necessary to prevent burning.
4. **Serve:**
   - Transfer the cooked French toast to plates. Serve warm with a generous drizzle of maple syrup over the top.
5. **Garnish (Optional):**
   - Sprinkle with powdered sugar, top with fresh berries, or add a dollop of whipped cream for extra sweetness and flavor.
6. **Enjoy:**
   - Serve immediately and enjoy your delicious French toast with maple syrup while it's still warm and the syrup is nicely absorbed into the toast.

### Tips:

- Use slightly stale bread for French toast, as it absorbs the egg mixture better without becoming too soggy.
- You can customize your French toast by adding a dash of nutmeg or using different types of bread like challah or French bread.

- Keep cooked French toast warm by placing it on a baking sheet in a 200°F (93°C) oven while you finish cooking the rest.

This recipe is perfect for a leisurely weekend breakfast or brunch and is sure to satisfy with its rich, sweet flavors.

**Blueberry Muffins**

**Ingredients:**

- 1 and 1/2 cups all-purpose flour
- 3/4 cup granulated sugar
- 1/2 teaspoon salt
- 2 teaspoons baking powder
- 1/3 cup vegetable oil or melted butter
- 1 large egg
- 1/3 cup milk (whole milk or buttermilk preferred)
- 1 and 1/2 teaspoons vanilla extract
- 1 cup fresh or frozen blueberries (if using frozen, do not thaw)

**Instructions:**

1. **Preheat Oven and Prepare Muffin Pan:**
   - Preheat your oven to 375°F (190°C). Line a muffin pan with paper liners or grease each cup with butter or cooking spray.
2. **Mix Dry Ingredients:**
   - In a large bowl, whisk together the flour, sugar, salt, and baking powder until well combined.
3. **Combine Wet Ingredients:**
   - In a separate bowl, whisk together the vegetable oil or melted butter, egg, milk, and vanilla extract until smooth and well blended.
4. **Combine Wet and Dry Ingredients:**
   - Pour the wet ingredients into the bowl of dry ingredients. Stir gently with a spatula or wooden spoon until just combined. Do not overmix; it's okay if there are a few lumps in the batter.
5. **Fold in Blueberries:**
   - Gently fold the blueberries into the batter using a spatula. Be careful not to crush the berries too much.
6. **Fill Muffin Cups:**
   - Divide the batter evenly among the muffin cups, filling each about 2/3 full.
7. **Bake:**
   - Bake for 18-20 minutes, or until the tops of the muffins are golden brown and a toothpick inserted into the center comes out clean.
8. **Cool and Serve:**
   - Remove the muffins from the oven and let them cool in the pan for 5 minutes. Then, transfer them to a wire rack to cool completely, or enjoy them warm.
9. **Optional:**
   - You can sprinkle a little sugar on top of each muffin before baking for a crunchy topping, if desired.

**Tips:**

- If using frozen blueberries, toss them lightly with a tablespoon of flour before folding into the batter. This helps prevent them from sinking to the bottom of the muffins.
- Feel free to add lemon zest or a sprinkle of cinnamon to the batter for extra flavor.
- Store leftover muffins in an airtight container at room temperature for up to 3 days, or freeze them for longer storage.

These homemade blueberry muffins are moist, tender, and bursting with juicy blueberries. They're a delightful treat for breakfast or any time of day!

## Breakfast Burrito with Sausage and Eggs

### Ingredients:

- 4 large flour tortillas
- 8 large eggs
- 1/2 pound breakfast sausage (pork or turkey), casings removed
- 1/2 cup shredded cheddar cheese (or your favorite cheese)
- 1/4 cup diced onion
- 1/4 cup diced bell pepper (any color)
- Salt and pepper, to taste
- Salsa, sour cream, or hot sauce for serving (optional)

### Instructions:

1. **Cook the Sausage:**
    - Heat a large skillet over medium heat. Add the breakfast sausage, breaking it up with a spatula or wooden spoon as it cooks. Cook until the sausage is browned and cooked through, about 5-7 minutes. Remove from skillet and set aside.
2. **Prepare the Eggs:**
    - In the same skillet, add a little oil if needed and sauté the diced onion and bell pepper until softened, about 3-4 minutes.
    - In a bowl, whisk the eggs together with salt and pepper to taste. Pour the eggs into the skillet with the onion and bell pepper. Cook, stirring occasionally, until the eggs are scrambled and cooked through.
3. **Assemble the Burritos:**
    - Warm the flour tortillas in the microwave or in a dry skillet for a few seconds to make them pliable.
    - Divide the scrambled eggs, cooked sausage, and shredded cheese evenly among the tortillas, placing the filling in the center of each tortilla.
4. **Fold the Burritos:**
    - Fold the sides of the tortilla over the filling, then fold the bottom edge up and roll tightly to form a burrito.
5. **Serve:**
    - Serve the breakfast burritos immediately while warm. You can serve them as is or with salsa, sour cream, or hot sauce on the side for dipping or drizzling.

### Tips:

- Customize your breakfast burritos with additional toppings such as diced tomatoes, avocado slices, or cilantro.
- Make-ahead tip: You can prepare the filling in advance and assemble the burritos right before serving. Wrap them tightly in foil and store in the refrigerator. Reheat in the oven or microwave before serving.
- For a healthier option, you can use whole wheat tortillas and turkey sausage.

This breakfast burrito recipe is versatile and can be adapted to your taste preferences. It's a great way to enjoy a filling and delicious breakfast on the go or at home!

# Greek Yogurt Parfait with Fresh Berries

**Ingredients:**

- 1 cup Greek yogurt (plain or flavored, such as vanilla)
- 1 cup fresh berries (such as strawberries, blueberries, raspberries, or a mix)
- 1/4 cup granola (homemade or store-bought)
- 1 tablespoon honey (optional, for drizzling)
- Fresh mint leaves for garnish (optional)

**Instructions:**

1. **Prepare the Berries:**
   - Wash the fresh berries thoroughly under cold water. If using strawberries, hull and slice them.
2. **Layer the Parfait:**
   - In a clear glass or bowl, start by adding a layer of Greek yogurt at the bottom.
3. **Add Berries:**
   - Top the yogurt with a layer of fresh berries. You can use a variety of berries or focus on one type, depending on your preference.
4. **Add Granola:**
   - Sprinkle a layer of granola over the berries. This adds crunch and texture to the parfait.
5. **Repeat Layers:**
   - Repeat the layers of Greek yogurt, berries, and granola until you reach the top of the glass or bowl. The order of layers is flexible, so feel free to adjust based on your preference.
6. **Finish with Berries and Garnish:**
   - Top the parfait with a few extra berries and drizzle with honey, if desired, for added sweetness.
7. **Garnish (Optional):**
   - Garnish with fresh mint leaves for a pop of color and extra freshness.
8. **Serve Immediately:**
   - Serve the Greek yogurt parfait immediately while the granola is still crunchy and the berries are fresh.

**Tips:**

- Customize your parfait by adding layers of nuts, seeds, or dried fruits for additional flavor and nutrition.
- For a sweeter parfait, you can use flavored Greek yogurt or mix honey into plain Greek yogurt before layering.
- Make-ahead tip: You can prepare the components of the parfait separately and assemble just before serving to keep the granola crunchy.

This Greek yogurt parfait with fresh berries is not only delicious but also packed with protein, vitamins, and fiber, making it a nutritious choice for breakfast or a satisfying snack any time of day.

**Scrambled Eggs with Smoked Salmon**

**Ingredients:**

- 4 large eggs
- 1/4 cup milk or cream
- Salt and pepper, to taste
- 2 tablespoons unsalted butter
- 3 ounces smoked salmon, chopped or thinly sliced
- Fresh chives or dill, chopped (optional, for garnish)
- Toast or bagels, for serving (optional)

**Instructions:**

1. **Prepare the Eggs:**
   - In a bowl, whisk together the eggs, milk or cream, salt, and pepper until well combined. Whisking with a fork or whisk until the mixture is uniform.
2. **Cook the Eggs:**
   - Heat a non-stick skillet over medium heat. Add the butter and let it melt and start to sizzle.
   - Pour the egg mixture into the skillet. Let it sit for a few seconds until the edges start to set.
   - Using a spatula, gently stir the eggs from the edges towards the center. Continue stirring occasionally until the eggs are mostly set but still slightly runny.
3. **Add the Smoked Salmon:**
   - Add the chopped or thinly sliced smoked salmon to the skillet with the scrambled eggs. Gently fold the salmon into the eggs until evenly distributed. Cook for another minute or until the eggs are fully cooked and the salmon is warmed through.
4. **Serve:**
   - Transfer the scrambled eggs with smoked salmon to plates. Sprinkle with chopped fresh chives or dill, if using, for garnish.
5. **Optional Serving Suggestion:**
   - Serve the scrambled eggs with smoked salmon on toasted bread or bagels for a complete meal. You can also serve it with a side salad or fresh fruit.

**Tips:**

- Be cautious with adding additional salt as smoked salmon can be quite salty already. Taste and adjust seasoning accordingly.
- For extra creaminess, you can add a dollop of cream cheese or crème fraîche to the eggs just before serving.
- If you prefer softer scrambled eggs, cook them over lower heat and stir gently and more frequently.

This scrambled eggs with smoked salmon recipe is quick to prepare and offers a luxurious twist to traditional scrambled eggs. It's sure to impress your guests or make any breakfast feel special!

# Cinnamon Rolls with Cream Cheese Frosting

**Ingredients:**

*For the dough:*

- 4 cups all-purpose flour
- 1/3 cup granulated sugar
- 1 teaspoon salt
- 2 and 1/4 teaspoons instant yeast (or one packet)
- 1 cup milk (whole milk is preferred)
- 6 tablespoons unsalted butter, softened
- 2 large eggs

*For the filling:*

- 1/2 cup unsalted butter, softened
- 1 cup brown sugar, packed
- 2 tablespoons ground cinnamon

*For the cream cheese frosting:*

- 4 ounces cream cheese, softened
- 1/4 cup unsalted butter, softened
- 1 cup powdered sugar
- 1/2 teaspoon vanilla extract

**Instructions:**

1. **Make the Dough:**
    - In a large mixing bowl or the bowl of a stand mixer fitted with a dough hook, combine 3 cups of flour, sugar, salt, and instant yeast.
    - In a small saucepan or microwave-safe bowl, heat the milk and butter until the butter is melted and the mixture is warm (about 120-130°F or 50-55°C).
    - Add the milk mixture and eggs to the dry ingredients. Mix until well combined.
    - Gradually add the remaining 1 cup of flour, mixing until the dough comes together and pulls away from the sides of the bowl.
    - Knead the dough for about 5-7 minutes by hand on a lightly floured surface, or continue kneading with the dough hook for 5 minutes on medium speed, until the dough is smooth and elastic.
2. **Let the Dough Rise:**
    - Place the dough in a greased bowl, turning once to coat. Cover with plastic wrap or a clean kitchen towel and let it rise in a warm, draft-free place for about 1 hour, or until doubled in size.
3. **Prepare the Filling:**

- In a small bowl, mix together the softened butter, brown sugar, and ground cinnamon until smooth and well combined.
4. **Roll and Fill the Dough:**
    - Punch down the risen dough and roll it out on a lightly floured surface into a rectangle, about 16x12 inches.
    - Spread the cinnamon filling evenly over the dough, leaving a small border around the edges.
5. **Roll Up the Dough:**
    - Starting from one long edge, tightly roll up the dough into a log. Pinch the seam to seal.
6. **Cut the Rolls:**
    - Using a sharp knife or unflavored dental floss, cut the log into 12 equal slices.
7. **Arrange in Pan and Rise Again:**
    - Place the slices into a greased 9x13-inch baking pan or two 9-inch round pans, spacing them evenly. Cover with plastic wrap or a kitchen towel and let them rise again in a warm place for about 30-45 minutes, or until doubled in size.
8. **Bake the Rolls:**
    - Preheat your oven to 375°F (190°C). Bake the cinnamon rolls for 20-25 minutes, or until they are golden brown.
9. **Make the Cream Cheese Frosting:**
    - While the rolls are baking, prepare the cream cheese frosting. In a mixing bowl, beat together the softened cream cheese and butter until smooth and creamy.
    - Add the powdered sugar and vanilla extract, and beat until well combined and smooth.
10. **Frost the Rolls:**
    - Remove the cinnamon rolls from the oven and let them cool slightly in the pan for about 5 minutes.
    - Spread the cream cheese frosting over the warm rolls while they are still in the pan.
11. **Serve and Enjoy:**
    - Serve the cinnamon rolls warm. Pull them apart and enjoy the gooey, cinnamon-spiced goodness with the creamy frosting.

**Tips:**

- If you prefer a thicker frosting, you can adjust the amount of powdered sugar or cream cheese to your liking.
- For extra flavor, you can add a pinch of nutmeg or a dash of lemon juice to the cream cheese frosting.
- These cinnamon rolls are best enjoyed fresh on the day they are baked, but you can store leftovers in an airtight container at room temperature for up to 2 days, or in the refrigerator for up to 5 days.

These homemade cinnamon rolls with cream cheese frosting are sure to impress with their soft, fluffy texture and irresistible cinnamon aroma. They're a delightful treat for any occasion!

**Veggie Omelette**

**Ingredients:**

- 3 large eggs
- 1/4 cup diced bell peppers (any color)
- 1/4 cup diced onion
- 1/4 cup diced tomatoes
- 1/4 cup sliced mushrooms
- Handful of spinach leaves
- Salt and pepper, to taste
- 1 tablespoon butter or oil
- 1/4 cup shredded cheese (optional)
- Fresh herbs, such as parsley or chives, for garnish (optional)

**Instructions:**

1. **Prepare the Veggies:**
   - Heat a non-stick skillet over medium heat. Add a little butter or oil.
   - Sauté the diced bell peppers, onions, tomatoes, and mushrooms until they are softened and lightly browned, about 3-4 minutes. Add the spinach leaves and cook until wilted. Season with salt and pepper to taste. Remove from the skillet and set aside.
2. **Whisk the Eggs:**
   - In a bowl, crack the eggs and whisk them together until well combined. Season with a pinch of salt and pepper.
3. **Cook the Omelette:**
   - Return the skillet to medium heat and add a little more butter or oil if needed, swirling to coat the pan evenly.
   - Pour the whisked eggs into the skillet. Let them cook undisturbed for a few seconds until the edges start to set.
4. **Add the Veggies:**
   - Once the edges of the eggs begin to set, sprinkle the sautéed vegetables evenly over one half of the omelette.
5. **Optional Cheese:**
   - Sprinkle shredded cheese over the veggies if using.
6. **Fold the Omelette:**
   - Use a spatula to carefully fold the other half of the omelette over the vegetables and cheese. Press gently with the spatula to seal.
7. **Finish Cooking:**
   - Cook for another 1-2 minutes until the omelette is cooked through and the cheese is melted, adjusting the heat as needed to prevent burning.
8. **Serve:**
   - Slide the veggie omelette onto a plate. Garnish with fresh herbs, if desired.

**Tips:**

- You can customize your veggie omelette with any vegetables you like or have on hand such as zucchini, broccoli, or even leftover roasted vegetables.
- For extra protein, you can add cooked diced ham, bacon, or crumbled sausage to the omelette.
- Serve your veggie omelette with a side of toast, fresh fruit, or a simple green salad for a complete meal.

This veggie omelette is nutritious, versatile, and perfect for a quick and satisfying breakfast or brunch. Enjoy experimenting with different vegetable combinations to suit your taste!

**Banana Pancakes with Nutella**

**Ingredients:**

- 1 cup all-purpose flour
- 1 tablespoon granulated sugar
- 1 teaspoon baking powder
- 1/2 teaspoon baking soda
- 1/4 teaspoon salt
- 1 cup milk
- 1 large egg
- 2 ripe bananas, mashed
- 2 tablespoons unsalted butter, melted
- Nutella, for serving
- Sliced bananas, for garnish (optional)
- Maple syrup, for serving (optional)

**Instructions:**

1. **Prepare the Dry Ingredients:**
   - In a large bowl, whisk together the flour, sugar, baking powder, baking soda, and salt until well combined.
2. **Prepare the Wet Ingredients:**
   - In another bowl, whisk together the milk, egg, mashed bananas, and melted butter until smooth.
3. **Combine Wet and Dry Ingredients:**
   - Pour the wet ingredients into the bowl with the dry ingredients. Stir gently with a spatula until just combined. Be careful not to overmix; it's okay if there are a few lumps in the batter.
4. **Cook the Pancakes:**
   - Heat a non-stick skillet or griddle over medium heat. Lightly grease the surface with butter or cooking spray.
   - Pour about 1/4 cup of batter onto the skillet for each pancake. Cook until bubbles form on the surface of the pancake and the edges look set, about 2-3 minutes.
5. **Flip and Cook:**
   - Carefully flip the pancakes with a spatula and cook until golden brown on the other side, about 1-2 minutes more.
6. **Serve:**
   - Stack the banana pancakes on a plate. Spread a generous amount of Nutella between each pancake layer and on top.
   - Garnish with sliced bananas, if desired. Drizzle with maple syrup for extra sweetness, if desired.
7. **Enjoy:**
   - Serve the banana pancakes with Nutella warm and enjoy the delicious combination of flavors!

**Tips:**

- Make sure to use ripe bananas for the best flavor and sweetness in the pancakes.
- Adjust the amount of Nutella according to your preference for sweetness and chocolate flavor.
- You can keep the cooked pancakes warm in a 200°F (93°C) oven while you finish cooking the rest.

These banana pancakes with Nutella are sure to be a hit at breakfast or brunch, combining the comforting taste of pancakes with the indulgent flavor of Nutella and bananas. Enjoy them as a special treat for any occasion!

**Chia Seed Pudding with Almond Milk**

**Ingredients:**

- 1/4 cup chia seeds
- 1 cup almond milk (unsweetened)
- 1 tablespoon maple syrup or honey (optional, for sweetness)
- 1/2 teaspoon vanilla extract
- Fresh berries, sliced fruits, or nuts for topping (optional)

**Instructions:**

1. **Mix Chia Seeds and Almond Milk:**
   - In a bowl or jar, combine the chia seeds and almond milk. Stir well to mix thoroughly. Make sure there are no clumps of chia seeds.
2. **Add Sweetener and Vanilla:**
   - If desired, stir in maple syrup or honey for sweetness and vanilla extract for flavor. Mix well.
3. **Let it Set:**
   - Cover the bowl or jar and refrigerate for at least 2 hours, or preferably overnight. The chia seeds will absorb the almond milk and thicken to a pudding-like consistency.
4. **Stir Occasionally (Optional):**
   - If you remember, you can stir the mixture again after about 30 minutes to prevent clumping and ensure even distribution of chia seeds.
5. **Serve:**
   - Once the chia seed pudding has set and reached the desired consistency, give it a good stir. If it's too thick, you can add a little more almond milk to thin it out.
6. **Top and Enjoy:**
   - Serve the chia seed pudding in bowls or jars. Top with fresh berries, sliced fruits, or nuts for added flavor, texture, and nutrition.

**Tips:**

- Customize your chia seed pudding with various toppings such as coconut flakes, granola, or a drizzle of nut butter.
- Adjust the sweetness by adding more or less maple syrup or honey according to your preference.
- Chia seed pudding can be stored in the refrigerator for up to 5 days, making it a convenient make-ahead breakfast or snack option.

Chia seed pudding with almond milk is not only easy to prepare but also packed with fiber, omega-3 fatty acids, and other nutrients, making it a healthy and satisfying choice to start your day or enjoy as a wholesome snack.

# Breakfast Quesadilla with Cheese and Bacon

## Ingredients:

- 2 large flour tortillas
- 1 cup shredded cheese (cheddar, Monterey Jack, or your favorite melting cheese)
- 4 slices bacon, cooked and crumbled
- 2 large eggs
- Salt and pepper, to taste
- Butter or oil, for cooking

## Optional Additions:

- Diced bell peppers, onions, or tomatoes
- Salsa, sour cream, or guacamole for serving
- Fresh herbs like cilantro or green onions for garnish

## Instructions:

1. **Cook the Bacon:**
   - In a skillet over medium heat, cook the bacon until crispy. Transfer to a paper towel-lined plate to drain excess grease. Once cooled, crumble or chop into small pieces.
2. **Prepare the Eggs:**
   - In a bowl, whisk the eggs with a pinch of salt and pepper until well combined.
   - Heat a non-stick skillet over medium heat and add a small amount of butter or oil. Pour in the eggs and cook, stirring gently with a spatula, until they are scrambled and cooked through. Remove from heat.
3. **Assemble the Quesadilla:**
   - Place one tortilla on a clean surface. Sprinkle half of the shredded cheese evenly over the tortilla.
   - Spread the cooked scrambled eggs evenly over the cheese.
   - Sprinkle the crumbled bacon on top of the eggs.
   - Sprinkle the remaining cheese over the bacon.
   - Place the second tortilla on top to cover the filling.
4. **Cook the Quesadilla:**
   - Heat a skillet or griddle over medium heat. Carefully transfer the assembled quesadilla to the skillet.
   - Cook for 2-3 minutes on each side, pressing down gently with a spatula, until the tortilla is golden brown and the cheese is melted.
5. **Serve:**
   - Remove the quesadilla from the skillet and transfer to a cutting board. Let it cool for a minute before slicing into wedges with a sharp knife.
   - Serve hot with salsa, sour cream, guacamole, or your favorite toppings on the side.

**Tips:**

- Customize your breakfast quesadilla with additional ingredients such as diced bell peppers, onions, or tomatoes for extra flavor and nutrition.
- Use a combination of cheeses for added flavor complexity.
- For a quicker option, you can use pre-cooked bacon or bacon bits.
- You can also make a larger quesadilla using larger tortillas and adjusting the ingredient quantities accordingly.

This breakfast quesadilla with cheese and bacon is a hearty and satisfying meal that's perfect for any morning. Enjoy the combination of melted cheese, crispy bacon, and fluffy scrambled eggs in every bite!

## Sourdough Toast with Avocado and Tomato

### Ingredients:

- 2 slices of sourdough bread
- 1 ripe avocado
- 1 medium tomato, thinly sliced
- Salt and pepper, to taste
- Red pepper flakes (optional)
- Fresh lemon juice (optional)
- Fresh basil leaves or cilantro, chopped (optional)

### Instructions:

1. **Toast the Sourdough Bread:**
   - Toast the sourdough bread slices until they are golden brown and crispy. You can use a toaster or a toaster oven for this step.
2. **Prepare the Avocado:**
   - While the bread is toasting, cut the avocado in half and remove the pit. Scoop the flesh into a small bowl.
3. **Mash the Avocado:**
   - Mash the avocado with a fork until smooth or leave it slightly chunky, depending on your preference. If desired, squeeze a little fresh lemon juice over the mashed avocado to prevent browning and add a hint of citrus flavor.
4. **Assemble the Toast:**
   - Spread the mashed avocado evenly onto each slice of toasted sourdough bread.
5. **Add Tomato Slices:**
   - Arrange the thinly sliced tomatoes on top of the mashed avocado. Season with salt and pepper to taste.
6. **Optional Garnishes:**
   - Sprinkle red pepper flakes for a touch of heat, or garnish with chopped fresh basil leaves or cilantro for added freshness and flavor.
7. **Serve and Enjoy:**
   - Serve the sourdough toast with avocado and tomato immediately while the toast is still warm and crispy.

### Tips:

- Choose ripe avocados for the best texture and flavor. They should yield slightly to gentle pressure when ripe.
- You can customize your avocado toast by adding other toppings such as a poached egg, crumbled feta cheese, or a drizzle of balsamic glaze.
- Sourdough bread adds a tangy flavor and hearty texture to this dish, but you can use any bread you prefer.

This sourdough toast with avocado and tomato is not only delicious but also packed with healthy fats, vitamins, and minerals, making it a satisfying and nutritious choice for breakfast or a quick snack. Enjoy it any time of day!

**Belgian Waffles with Strawberries and Whipped Cream**

**Ingredients:**

*For the Belgian Waffles:*

- 2 cups all-purpose flour
- 1/4 cup granulated sugar
- 1 tablespoon baking powder
- 1/2 teaspoon salt
- 1 and 3/4 cups milk
- 2 large eggs
- 1/2 cup unsalted butter, melted
- 1 teaspoon vanilla extract

*For Topping:*

- Fresh strawberries, sliced
- Whipped cream (homemade or store-bought)
- Maple syrup or honey (optional, for drizzling)
- Powdered sugar, for dusting (optional)

**Instructions:**

1. **Preheat and Prep Waffle Iron:**
   - Preheat your Belgian waffle iron according to manufacturer's instructions. Lightly grease the iron if necessary to prevent sticking.
2. **Mix Dry Ingredients:**
   - In a large bowl, whisk together the flour, sugar, baking powder, and salt until well combined.
3. **Combine Wet Ingredients:**
   - In another bowl, whisk together the milk, eggs, melted butter, and vanilla extract until smooth.
4. **Make Waffle Batter:**
   - Pour the wet ingredients into the bowl with the dry ingredients. Stir gently until just combined. It's okay if there are a few lumps in the batter; do not overmix.
5. **Cook Waffles:**
   - Pour enough batter onto the preheated waffle iron to cover the grids. Close the iron and cook according to the manufacturer's instructions until the waffles are golden brown and crispy.
6. **Prepare Toppings:**
   - While the waffles are cooking, wash and slice fresh strawberries. Prepare whipped cream if making homemade or have store-bought whipped cream ready.
7. **Serve:**

- Once cooked, transfer the Belgian waffles to plates. Top each waffle with sliced strawberries and a generous dollop of whipped cream.
8. **Optional Garnish:**
   - Drizzle with maple syrup or honey for extra sweetness if desired. Dust with powdered sugar for an elegant finish.
9. **Enjoy:**
   - Serve the Belgian waffles with strawberries and whipped cream immediately while warm.

**Tips:**

- For extra flavor, you can add a pinch of cinnamon or nutmeg to the waffle batter.
- If making whipped cream at home, whip cold heavy cream with a whisk or mixer until soft peaks form. Add a bit of sugar and vanilla extract to taste.
- Belgian waffles are best enjoyed fresh and warm, but you can keep them warm in a 200°F (93°C) oven while cooking the rest.

This recipe for Belgian waffles with strawberries and whipped cream is sure to impress with its combination of crisp waffles, juicy strawberries, and airy whipped cream. It's perfect for a special breakfast or brunch occasion!

# Breakfast Hash with Potatoes and Chorizo

## Ingredients:

- 1 lb potatoes (about 2-3 medium potatoes), peeled and diced into 1/2-inch cubes
- 8 oz chorizo sausage, casing removed and crumbled (you can use Mexican or Spanish chorizo)
- 1 small onion, diced
- 1 bell pepper (any color), diced
- 2 cloves garlic, minced
- 1 teaspoon paprika
- 1/2 teaspoon cumin
- Salt and pepper, to taste
- 2 tablespoons olive oil
- 4 eggs (optional, for serving)
- Fresh cilantro or parsley, chopped (for garnish)

## Instructions:

1. **Cook the Potatoes:**
   - Heat 1 tablespoon of olive oil in a large skillet over medium heat. Add the diced potatoes in a single layer. Cook, stirring occasionally, until the potatoes are golden brown and crispy on the outside and tender on the inside, about 15-20 minutes. Season with salt and pepper. Remove the potatoes from the skillet and set aside.
2. **Cook the Chorizo and Vegetables:**
   - In the same skillet, add the crumbled chorizo. Cook over medium heat, breaking it apart with a spoon, until it is browned and cooked through, about 5-7 minutes. Remove the cooked chorizo from the skillet and set aside.
   - Add the remaining tablespoon of olive oil to the skillet. Add the diced onion and bell pepper. Cook, stirring occasionally, until softened, about 5 minutes.
3. **Combine and Season:**
   - Return the cooked potatoes and chorizo to the skillet with the vegetables. Add minced garlic, paprika, cumin, and additional salt and pepper to taste. Stir well to combine all ingredients evenly. Cook for another 2-3 minutes to allow the flavors to meld together.
4. **Optional: Cook Eggs (for serving):**
   - If desired, you can fry, poach, or scramble eggs separately to serve on top of the breakfast hash. This adds a delicious and creamy texture to the dish.
5. **Serve:**
   - Divide the breakfast hash among serving plates. Top each serving with a cooked egg, if using. Garnish with chopped fresh cilantro or parsley for added freshness and color.

## Tips:

- Adjust the spiciness of the dish by using mild or spicy chorizo according to your preference.
- You can customize the vegetables in the hash based on what you have on hand or your personal taste. Mushrooms, spinach, or diced tomatoes also work well.
- Serve the breakfast hash with a side of toast, avocado slices, or salsa for a complete meal.

This breakfast hash with potatoes and chorizo is a comforting and satisfying dish that's perfect for a weekend brunch or any time you want a hearty breakfast. Enjoy the combination of crispy potatoes, flavorful chorizo, and vibrant vegetables!

# Spinach and Feta Quiche

**Ingredients:**

- 1 pie crust (store-bought or homemade)
- 5 large eggs
- 1 cup milk or half-and-half
- 1 cup fresh spinach, chopped
- 1/2 cup crumbled feta cheese
- 1/2 cup shredded mozzarella cheese (optional)
- 1/4 cup grated Parmesan cheese
- 1/2 small onion, finely chopped
- 2 cloves garlic, minced
- 1 tablespoon olive oil
- Salt and pepper, to taste
- Pinch of nutmeg (optional)

**Instructions:**

1. **Preheat the Oven:**
    - Preheat your oven to 375°F (190°C).
2. **Prepare the Pie Crust:**
    - If using a store-bought pie crust, place it in a pie dish and crimp the edges. If using homemade, roll out the dough and fit it into a pie dish, crimping the edges as desired. Prick the bottom of the crust with a fork.
3. **Prepare the Spinach:**
    - Heat olive oil in a skillet over medium heat. Add chopped onion and minced garlic, cooking until softened and fragrant, about 3-4 minutes.
    - Add chopped spinach to the skillet and cook until wilted, about 2-3 minutes. Remove from heat and set aside.
4. **Prepare the Egg Mixture:**
    - In a mixing bowl, whisk together eggs and milk (or half-and-half) until well combined. Season with salt, pepper, and a pinch of nutmeg if desired.
5. **Assemble the Quiche:**
    - Spread the sautéed spinach mixture evenly over the bottom of the pie crust.
    - Sprinkle crumbled feta cheese, shredded mozzarella (if using), and grated Parmesan cheese over the spinach.
6. **Pour the Egg Mixture:**
    - Carefully pour the egg and milk mixture over the spinach and cheese filling in the pie crust. Use a spoon to gently distribute the filling evenly.
7. **Bake the Quiche:**
    - Place the quiche in the preheated oven and bake for 35-40 minutes, or until the top is golden brown and the center is set. The quiche is done when a knife inserted into the center comes out clean.
8. **Cool and Serve:**

- Allow the quiche to cool for a few minutes before slicing and serving. Garnish with fresh herbs like parsley or chives if desired.

**Tips:**

- You can customize this quiche by adding other vegetables like mushrooms or bell peppers.
- For a crustless version, simply skip the pie crust and pour the filling directly into a greased pie dish.
- Quiche can be served warm or at room temperature. Store any leftovers in the refrigerator and reheat gently in the oven or microwave.

This spinach and feta quiche is flavorful, creamy, and makes for a satisfying meal. It's perfect for gatherings or a cozy meal at home, offering a wonderful blend of spinach, tangy feta cheese, and savory egg custard in every bite.

# Oatmeal with Caramelized Bananas

## Ingredients:

- 1 cup old-fashioned oats
- 2 cups water (or milk for a creamier texture)
- Pinch of salt
- 2 ripe bananas, sliced
- 2 tablespoons butter
- 2 tablespoons brown sugar (adjust to taste)
- 1/2 teaspoon ground cinnamon
- Optional toppings: chopped nuts (like walnuts or pecans), raisins, a drizzle of honey or maple syrup

## Instructions:

1. **Cook the Oatmeal:**
   - In a medium saucepan, bring the water (or milk) and a pinch of salt to a boil.
   - Stir in the oats and reduce the heat to medium-low. Cook, stirring occasionally, for about 5-7 minutes or until the oats are creamy and tender. Remove from heat and cover to keep warm.
2. **Caramelize the Bananas:**
   - While the oatmeal is cooking, heat a skillet over medium heat. Add the butter and let it melt.
   - Add the sliced bananas to the skillet and sprinkle with brown sugar and ground cinnamon.
   - Cook the bananas for 2-3 minutes on each side, or until they are caramelized and golden brown. Be careful not to stir them too much; allow them to caramelize undisturbed on each side.
3. **Serve:**
   - Divide the cooked oatmeal into bowls.
   - Top each bowl with the caramelized bananas, along with any pan juices from caramelizing.
   - Optional: Add toppings like chopped nuts, raisins, or a drizzle of honey or maple syrup for extra flavor and texture.
4. **Enjoy:**
   - Serve the oatmeal with caramelized bananas warm and enjoy the creamy oats with the sweet and caramelized banana slices.

## Tips:

- For extra creamy oatmeal, use milk instead of water.
- Adjust the sweetness of the caramelized bananas by varying the amount of brown sugar used.
- You can also add vanilla extract to the oatmeal while cooking for additional flavor.

- Feel free to customize your oatmeal with other toppings like fresh berries, shredded coconut, or a dollop of yogurt.

This oatmeal with caramelized bananas is a comforting and nutritious breakfast choice that's sure to warm you up on a chilly morning. The combination of creamy oats and sweet bananas makes it a delightful treat to start your day!

## Bagel with Lox and Cream Cheese

### Ingredients:

- 1 bagel (plain, sesame, or everything)
- Cream cheese (to taste)
- Smoked salmon (lox), thinly sliced
- Red onion, thinly sliced (optional)
- Capers (optional)
- Fresh dill, chopped (optional)
- Lemon wedges (optional)

### Instructions:

1. **Prepare the Bagel:**
    - Slice the bagel in half horizontally. If desired, lightly toast the bagel halves until they are warm and slightly crispy.
2. **Spread Cream Cheese:**
    - Spread a generous amount of cream cheese on each half of the bagel. Use as much or as little as you prefer.
3. **Add Smoked Salmon (Lox):**
    - Arrange the thinly sliced smoked salmon (lox) evenly over the cream cheese on both bagel halves.
4. **Optional Toppings:**
    - Top the smoked salmon with thinly sliced red onion, capers, and chopped fresh dill for extra flavor and texture. These toppings complement the flavors of the smoked salmon and cream cheese.
5. **Serve:**
    - Close the bagel halves together to form a sandwich. Serve immediately, optionally with lemon wedges on the side for squeezing over the lox.

### Tips:

- Choose a high-quality bagel and smoked salmon for the best flavor experience.
- You can customize your bagel with lox and cream cheese by adding sliced tomatoes, cucumber slices, or lettuce for extra freshness.
- Serve with a side of fresh fruit, such as sliced oranges or berries, to balance the savory flavors.

This bagel with lox and cream cheese is a delicious and satisfying meal that's perfect for breakfast or brunch. Enjoy the combination of creamy, salty, and savory flavors in every bite!

# Breakfast Tacos with Chorizo and Egg

**Ingredients:**

- 6 small flour or corn tortillas
- 8 oz chorizo sausage, casing removed and crumbled
- 4 large eggs
- Salt and pepper, to taste
- 1/2 cup shredded cheese (cheddar, Monterey Jack, or your favorite melting cheese)
- 1 avocado, sliced (optional)
- Salsa, pico de gallo, or hot sauce for serving
- Fresh cilantro, chopped (optional)

**Instructions:**

1. **Cook the Chorizo:**
   - Heat a skillet over medium heat. Add the crumbled chorizo sausage to the skillet and cook, breaking it apart with a spoon, until it is browned and cooked through, about 5-7 minutes. Remove excess fat if necessary.
2. **Scramble the Eggs:**
   - In a bowl, whisk the eggs with a pinch of salt and pepper until well combined.
   - Push the chorizo to one side of the skillet and pour the beaten eggs into the empty side. Cook, stirring gently with a spatula, until the eggs are scrambled and cooked through, about 3-4 minutes. Mix the chorizo and eggs together in the skillet.
3. **Warm the Tortillas:**
   - Heat the tortillas in a separate skillet or in the microwave until they are warm and pliable.
4. **Assemble the Tacos:**
   - Divide the chorizo and egg mixture evenly among the warmed tortillas.
   - Sprinkle shredded cheese over the chorizo and egg mixture.
5. **Add Optional Toppings:**
   - Top each taco with sliced avocado, salsa, pico de gallo, or hot sauce according to your preference.
   - Garnish with chopped fresh cilantro for extra freshness and flavor.
6. **Serve:**
   - Serve the breakfast tacos immediately while warm. Enjoy the delicious combination of flavors and textures!

**Tips:**

- Customize your breakfast tacos with additional toppings such as diced tomatoes, diced onions, or a dollop of sour cream.
- For a healthier option, you can use turkey chorizo or chicken chorizo instead of pork chorizo.

- Serve with a side of refried beans, Mexican rice, or a fresh fruit salad for a complete meal.

These breakfast tacos with chorizo and egg are quick to make and packed with savory flavors, making them perfect for a hearty breakfast or brunch. Enjoy them any time of day for a satisfying meal!

# Lemon Ricotta Pancakes

**Ingredients:**

- 1 cup all-purpose flour
- 2 tablespoons granulated sugar
- 1 teaspoon baking powder
- 1/2 teaspoon baking soda
- 1/4 teaspoon salt
- 1 cup ricotta cheese (whole milk or part-skim)
- 3/4 cup milk
- 2 large eggs, separated
- Zest of 1 lemon
- Juice of 1 lemon
- 1 teaspoon vanilla extract
- Butter or oil, for cooking

**Instructions:**

1. **Prepare Dry Ingredients:**
   - In a large bowl, whisk together the flour, sugar, baking powder, baking soda, and salt until well combined.
2. **Prepare Wet Ingredients:**
   - In another bowl, whisk together the ricotta cheese, milk, egg yolks, lemon zest, lemon juice, and vanilla extract until smooth.
3. **Combine Wet and Dry Ingredients:**
   - Pour the wet ingredients into the bowl with the dry ingredients. Stir gently until just combined. The batter may be slightly lumpy, which is okay. Avoid overmixing.
4. **Whip Egg Whites (Optional Step for Fluffier Pancakes):**
   - In a separate clean bowl, using a hand mixer or stand mixer, beat the egg whites until stiff peaks form.
5. **Fold in Egg Whites (if using):**
   - Gently fold the whipped egg whites into the pancake batter until just incorporated. This step adds airiness to the pancakes.
6. **Cook the Pancakes:**
   - Heat a non-stick skillet or griddle over medium heat. Add a small amount of butter or oil to coat the surface.
   - Pour about 1/4 cup of batter onto the skillet for each pancake. Cook until bubbles form on the surface of the pancake and the edges look set, about 2-3 minutes.
7. **Flip and Cook:**
   - Carefully flip the pancakes with a spatula and cook until golden brown on the other side, about 1-2 minutes more.
8. **Serve:**
   - Serve the lemon ricotta pancakes warm with your favorite toppings such as fresh berries, powdered sugar, maple syrup, or a dollop of whipped cream.

**Tips:**

- Use fresh ricotta cheese for the best texture and flavor.
- Adjust the amount of lemon zest and juice according to your preference for a more pronounced lemon flavor.
- Keep the cooked pancakes warm in a 200°F (93°C) oven while you finish cooking the rest.

These lemon ricotta pancakes are light, fluffy, and bursting with bright lemony flavor and creamy ricotta texture. They make a perfect breakfast or brunch treat for any occasion!

# Shakshuka (Eggs Poached in Spicy Tomato Sauce)

**Ingredients:**

- 2 tablespoons olive oil
- 1 onion, finely chopped
- 1 red bell pepper, seeded and chopped
- 3 cloves garlic, minced
- 1 teaspoon ground cumin
- 1 teaspoon smoked paprika
- 1/2 teaspoon ground coriander
- 1/4 teaspoon cayenne pepper (adjust to taste)
- 1 can (14 oz) crushed tomatoes
- 1 tablespoon tomato paste
- Salt and pepper, to taste
- 4-6 large eggs
- Fresh parsley or cilantro, chopped (for garnish)
- Crusty bread or pita, for serving

**Instructions:**

1. **Prepare the Sauce:**
   - Heat olive oil in a large skillet or cast-iron pan over medium heat. Add the chopped onion and red bell pepper. Cook, stirring occasionally, until softened, about 5-7 minutes.
2. **Add Garlic and Spices:**
   - Add minced garlic, ground cumin, smoked paprika, ground coriander, and cayenne pepper to the skillet. Cook for 1-2 minutes until fragrant.
3. **Add Tomatoes:**
   - Stir in the crushed tomatoes and tomato paste. Season with salt and pepper to taste. Simmer the sauce for 10-15 minutes, stirring occasionally, until it thickens slightly.
4. **Poach the Eggs:**
   - Using a spoon, create small indentations (or "wells") in the tomato sauce. Carefully crack one egg into each indentation. Season each egg with a pinch of salt and pepper.
5. **Cook the Eggs:**
   - Cover the skillet with a lid and let the eggs cook in the tomato sauce over medium-low heat for about 5-8 minutes, or until the egg whites are set and the yolks are still runny (or cooked to your desired doneness).
6. **Serve:**
   - Remove the skillet from heat. Sprinkle chopped fresh parsley or cilantro over the Shakshuka.
   - Serve immediately, straight from the skillet, with crusty bread or pita for dipping into the flavorful tomato sauce and scooping up the eggs.

**Tips:**

- Adjust the spiciness by varying the amount of cayenne pepper used.
- For a richer sauce, you can add a splash of water or broth while simmering.
- Shakshuka can be easily customized by adding other ingredients like feta cheese, olives, or spinach.
- Make sure to have enough bread for dipping into the sauce—it's part of the experience!

Shakshuka is a hearty and satisfying dish that's perfect for any meal of the day. Enjoy the combination of spicy tomato sauce and perfectly poached eggs for a flavorful culinary adventure!

**Breakfast Sandwich with Ham and Cheese**

**Ingredients:**

- 2 slices of bread (such as English muffins, sandwich bread, or bagels)
- 2 slices of ham (cooked)
- 2 slices of cheese (such as cheddar, Swiss, or American)
- 1 large egg
- Butter or oil for cooking
- Salt and pepper to taste

**Optional additions:**

- Sliced tomatoes
- Fresh spinach or lettuce
- Avocado slices
- Mayonnaise or mustard
- Hot sauce

**Instructions:**

1. **Prepare the Egg:**
    - Heat a non-stick skillet over medium heat and add a small amount of butter or oil.
    - Crack the egg into the skillet and cook to your preference (fried, scrambled, or even poached). Season with salt and pepper.
2. **Assemble the Sandwich:**
    - While the egg is cooking, lightly toast the bread slices if desired.
    - Layer one slice of bread with one slice of cheese, followed by the ham slices, and then the cooked egg. Add any optional additions like sliced tomatoes or avocado if desired.
    - Top with the remaining slice of cheese and the second slice of bread.
3. **Grill or Heat the Sandwich:**
    - Heat a panini press, sandwich press, or skillet over medium heat.
    - If using a panini press or sandwich press, place the assembled sandwich inside and cook according to the manufacturer's instructions until the bread is toasted and the cheese is melted.
    - If using a skillet, melt a little more butter or oil and place the sandwich in the skillet. Cook on each side for 2-3 minutes, pressing down gently with a spatula, until the bread is golden brown and the cheese is melted.
4. **Serve:**
    - Remove the breakfast sandwich from the heat and let it cool slightly before serving.
    - Cut the sandwich in half if desired and serve warm.

**Tips:**

- Customize your breakfast sandwich with your favorite cheese and bread. Whole grain or seeded breads add extra flavor and texture.
- For a healthier option, use lean ham or turkey slices.
- Add fresh herbs like parsley or chives to the egg for extra flavor.
- Wrap any leftovers tightly in foil or plastic wrap and store them in the refrigerator. Reheat in the oven or microwave for a quick breakfast on the go.

This breakfast sandwich with ham and cheese is quick to prepare and perfect for a satisfying morning meal. Enjoy it with a cup of coffee or juice for a delicious start to your day!

**Peanut Butter and Jelly Waffles**

**Ingredients:**

- 1 cup all-purpose flour
- 1 tablespoon granulated sugar
- 1 teaspoon baking powder
- 1/2 teaspoon baking soda
- 1/4 teaspoon salt
- 1 cup buttermilk (or substitute with 1 cup milk + 1 tablespoon lemon juice or vinegar, let sit for 5 minutes)
- 1/4 cup creamy peanut butter
- 1 large egg
- 2 tablespoons unsalted butter, melted
- 1/2 cup your favorite jelly or jam (such as strawberry, grape, or raspberry)
- Cooking spray or additional butter for greasing the waffle iron

**Instructions:**

1. **Preheat the Waffle Iron:**
   - Preheat your waffle iron according to the manufacturer's instructions.
2. **Prepare the Dry Ingredients:**
   - In a large bowl, whisk together the flour, sugar, baking powder, baking soda, and salt until well combined.
3. **Mix the Wet Ingredients:**
   - In another bowl, whisk together the buttermilk, creamy peanut butter, melted butter, and egg until smooth.
4. **Combine Wet and Dry Ingredients:**
   - Pour the wet ingredients into the bowl with the dry ingredients. Stir gently until just combined. The batter may be slightly lumpy, which is okay. Do not overmix.
5. **Cook the Waffles:**
   - Lightly grease the preheated waffle iron with cooking spray or brush with melted butter.
   - Pour enough batter onto the waffle iron to cover the grids. Close the iron and cook according to the manufacturer's instructions until the waffles are golden brown and crispy.
6. **Assemble the Waffles:**
   - Once cooked, carefully remove the waffles from the iron. Place them on a plate or wire rack.
7. **Serve:**
   - To serve, spread a generous amount of jelly or jam on top of each waffle. Optionally, spread a layer of peanut butter on the waffles before adding the jelly or jam for an extra peanut buttery flavor.
   - If desired, cut the waffles into quarters or halves for easier handling.
8. **Enjoy:**

- Serve the peanut butter and jelly waffles immediately while warm. They can be enjoyed as is or with additional toppings like fresh berries or a drizzle of honey.

**Tips:**

- For a crunchy texture, you can sprinkle chopped peanuts on top of the waffles before serving.
- Ensure the waffle iron is well-heated and properly greased to prevent sticking.
- Leftover waffles can be stored in an airtight container in the refrigerator for a few days or frozen for longer storage. Reheat in a toaster or toaster oven until warmed through.

These peanut butter and jelly waffles are a fun and tasty twist on a classic sandwich, perfect for breakfast or even as a sweet treat any time of day. Enjoy the nostalgic flavors in each bite!

**Huevos Rancheros**

**Ingredients:**

- 4 corn or flour tortillas
- 4 large eggs
- 1 cup refried beans (homemade or canned)
- 1 cup salsa (homemade or store-bought)
- 1 avocado, sliced
- Fresh cilantro, chopped (for garnish)
- Lime wedges (optional, for serving)
- Salt and pepper, to taste
- Optional toppings: shredded cheese, diced tomatoes, sour cream, jalapeños

**Instructions:**

1. **Warm the Tortillas:**
    - Heat the tortillas in a dry skillet or in the oven until they are warm and pliable. Keep them warm wrapped in a clean kitchen towel.
2. **Prepare the Eggs:**
    - In the same skillet, fry or scramble the eggs according to your preference. Season with salt and pepper.
3. **Warm the Refried Beans:**
    - Heat the refried beans in a small saucepan over medium heat until warmed through. Stir occasionally to prevent sticking.
4. **Assemble the Huevos Rancheros:**
    - Place a warm tortilla on each plate.
    - Spread a layer of warmed refried beans evenly over each tortilla.
    - Top each tortilla with a portion of salsa.
    - Place a fried or scrambled egg on top of each tortilla.
5. **Add Toppings:**
    - Garnish with sliced avocado, chopped cilantro, and any other optional toppings you like such as shredded cheese, diced tomatoes, or sour cream.
6. **Serve:**
    - Serve the Huevos Rancheros immediately, garnished with lime wedges on the side if desired.
    - Enjoy this hearty and flavorful breakfast dish with extra salsa or hot sauce on the side.

**Tips:**

- Customize your Huevos Rancheros by adding ingredients like chorizo, diced onions, or bell peppers to the eggs.
- For a healthier version, use whole wheat tortillas and low-fat refried beans.

- Make sure to have all your ingredients prepared and ready to assemble for a quick and delicious breakfast.

Huevos Rancheros is a delicious and satisfying breakfast that's sure to please. It's packed with flavor and makes for a hearty start to the day, combining the richness of eggs with the bold flavors of salsa and beans.

**Biscuits and Gravy**

**Ingredients:**

**For the Biscuits:**

- 2 cups all-purpose flour
- 1 tablespoon baking powder
- 1 teaspoon salt
- 1/2 cup cold unsalted butter, cubed
- 3/4 cup milk (plus more as needed)

**For the Sausage Gravy:**

- 1/2 lb breakfast sausage (pork or turkey)
- 1/4 cup all-purpose flour
- 3 cups whole milk
- Salt and pepper, to taste
- Pinch of cayenne pepper (optional, for heat)

**Instructions:**

**To Make the Biscuits:**

1. **Preheat the Oven:**
    - Preheat your oven to 450°F (230°C).
2. **Mix Dry Ingredients:**
    - In a large bowl, whisk together the flour, baking powder, and salt.
3. **Cut in Butter:**
    - Using a pastry cutter or your fingertips, cut the cold butter into the flour mixture until it resembles coarse crumbs.
4. **Add Milk:**
    - Gradually add the milk, stirring with a fork, until the dough just comes together and forms a sticky ball. Add a little more milk if necessary.
5. **Shape and Bake:**
    - Turn the dough out onto a lightly floured surface. Gently pat or roll the dough to about 1/2-inch thickness.
    - Using a biscuit cutter or the rim of a glass, cut out biscuits and place them on a baking sheet lined with parchment paper.
6. **Bake:**
    - Bake the biscuits in the preheated oven for 10-12 minutes, or until they are golden brown on top.

**To Make the Sausage Gravy:**

1. **Cook the Sausage:**

- In a large skillet or saucepan, cook the breakfast sausage over medium heat, breaking it apart with a spoon until it is browned and cooked through. Use a slotted spoon to transfer the cooked sausage to a plate, leaving the drippings in the pan.

2. **Make the Roux:**
   - Reduce the heat to medium-low. Sprinkle the flour into the sausage drippings in the skillet. Stir constantly for 1-2 minutes to cook the flour and form a roux.
3. **Add Milk:**
   - Gradually whisk in the milk, stirring constantly to prevent lumps. Bring the mixture to a simmer over medium heat.
4. **Thicken:**
   - Continue cooking and stirring until the gravy thickens, about 5-7 minutes. If the gravy becomes too thick, you can add more milk to reach your desired consistency.
5. **Season:**
   - Season the gravy with salt, pepper, and a pinch of cayenne pepper (if using), adjusting to taste.

## To Serve:

- Split open a warm biscuit and place it on a plate. Spoon generous amounts of the sausage gravy over the biscuit.
- Serve immediately, garnished with freshly ground black pepper if desired.

## Tips:

- For a shortcut, you can use store-bought biscuits or a biscuit mix instead of making them from scratch.
- If you prefer a spicier gravy, you can add a dash of hot sauce or a pinch of red pepper flakes along with the seasonings.
- Leftover biscuits and gravy can be stored separately in the refrigerator. Reheat the gravy gently on the stovetop, adding a splash of milk to thin it out if needed.

Enjoy this comforting and hearty Southern breakfast of biscuits and gravy, perfect for starting your day with a satisfying meal!

**Smoked Salmon Bagel with Cream Cheese**

**Ingredients:**

- 1 bagel (plain, sesame, or everything)
- Cream cheese (to taste)
- Smoked salmon slices
- Red onion, thinly sliced (optional)
- Capers (optional)
- Fresh dill, chopped (optional)
- Lemon wedges (optional)

**Instructions:**

1. **Prepare the Bagel:**
    - Slice the bagel in half horizontally.
2. **Spread Cream Cheese:**
    - Spread a generous amount of cream cheese on each half of the bagel.
3. **Add Smoked Salmon:**
    - Arrange the smoked salmon slices evenly on top of the cream cheese.
4. **Optional Toppings:**
    - Add thinly sliced red onion, capers, and chopped fresh dill on top of the smoked salmon for added flavor and texture.
5. **Serve:**
    - Squeeze a lemon wedge over the smoked salmon if desired.
    - Close the bagel halves together to form a sandwich.
6. **Enjoy:**
    - Serve the smoked salmon bagel immediately. It pairs well with a side of fresh fruit or a mixed greens salad.

**Tips:**

- Choose high-quality smoked salmon for the best flavor. You can use either cold-smoked or hot-smoked salmon depending on your preference.
- Customize your bagel with additional toppings like sliced cucumber, tomatoes, or avocado for extra freshness.
- For a richer flavor, you can add a sprinkle of black pepper or a dash of hot sauce to the cream cheese before assembling the bagel.

This smoked salmon bagel with cream cheese is a delicious and satisfying meal that's perfect for any time of day, whether you're enjoying a leisurely brunch or a quick breakfast on the go.

## Apple Cinnamon French Toast Bake

**Ingredients:**

- 1 loaf (about 14-16 oz) French bread, cut into 1-inch cubes
- 4-5 medium-sized apples, peeled, cored, and thinly sliced (such as Granny Smith or Honeycrisp)
- 6 large eggs
- 1 1/2 cups milk (whole milk or any milk of your choice)
- 1/2 cup heavy cream (optional, for a richer texture)
- 1/2 cup granulated sugar
- 1 tablespoon vanilla extract
- 1 teaspoon ground cinnamon
- 1/4 teaspoon ground nutmeg
- 1/4 teaspoon salt
- 1/2 cup brown sugar, packed
- 1/2 cup unsalted butter, melted
- Maple syrup, powdered sugar, or whipped cream (for serving)

**Instructions:**

1. **Prepare the Bread and Apples:**
    - Grease a 9x13-inch baking dish with butter or non-stick spray.
    - Arrange half of the bread cubes in the prepared baking dish. Top with half of the sliced apples.
    - Repeat with the remaining bread cubes and sliced apples.
2. **Prepare the Custard Mixture:**
    - In a large bowl, whisk together the eggs, milk, heavy cream (if using), granulated sugar, vanilla extract, cinnamon, nutmeg, and salt until well combined.
3. **Pour Custard Over Bread and Apples:**
    - Slowly pour the custard mixture over the bread and apples in the baking dish, making sure all the bread cubes are coated. Press down gently with a spatula to submerge the bread.
4. **Make the Topping:**
    - In a separate bowl, combine the brown sugar and melted butter. Stir until the mixture resembles wet sand.
5. **Assemble and Bake:**
    - Sprinkle the brown sugar and butter mixture evenly over the top of the French toast bake.
6. **Chill (Optional Step):**
    - Cover the baking dish with plastic wrap and refrigerate for at least 2 hours or overnight. This allows the bread to absorb the custard mixture.
7. **Bake:**
    - Preheat your oven to 350°F (175°C).

- Remove the plastic wrap from the baking dish. Bake the French toast bake in the preheated oven for 45-55 minutes, or until the top is golden brown and the center is set.

8. **Serve:**
   - Remove from the oven and let it cool slightly before serving.
   - Serve warm with maple syrup, a dusting of powdered sugar, or a dollop of whipped cream, if desired.

**Tips:**

- You can prepare the French toast bake the night before and refrigerate it overnight. Just remember to let it sit at room temperature for about 30 minutes before baking.
- Feel free to add chopped nuts (such as pecans or walnuts) to the topping mixture for extra crunch and flavor.
- Leftovers can be stored covered in the refrigerator for up to 2 days. Reheat in the oven or microwave before serving.

This apple cinnamon French toast bake is a wonderful make-ahead dish that's perfect for feeding a crowd or enjoying a cozy breakfast at home. The combination of apples, cinnamon, and custardy bread makes it a comforting and delicious treat!

# Breakfast Pizza with Eggs and Bacon

## Ingredients:

- 1 lb pizza dough (store-bought or homemade)
- 6 slices bacon, cooked until crispy and chopped
- 4 large eggs
- 1 cup shredded mozzarella cheese
- 1/2 cup shredded cheddar cheese
- 1/4 cup grated Parmesan cheese
- 1/2 cup tomato sauce or pizza sauce
- 1/2 teaspoon garlic powder
- Salt and pepper, to taste
- Fresh parsley or basil, chopped (for garnish)
- Red pepper flakes (optional, for added heat)

## Instructions:

1. **Preheat the Oven:**
    - Preheat your oven to 475°F (245°C). Place a pizza stone or baking sheet in the oven to preheat as well.
2. **Prepare the Dough:**
    - On a lightly floured surface, roll out the pizza dough to your desired thickness. Transfer the dough to a piece of parchment paper.
3. **Assemble the Pizza:**
    - Spread tomato sauce evenly over the pizza dough, leaving a small border around the edges.
    - Sprinkle garlic powder over the sauce.
    - Sprinkle mozzarella cheese evenly over the sauce
    - Scatter the chopped bacon over the cheese.
4. **Prepare the Eggs:**
    - Carefully crack the eggs onto the pizza, evenly spaced apart. You can crack them directly onto the pizza or crack them into a small bowl first and then slide them onto the pizza.
5. **Add Cheese and Seasoning:**
    - Sprinkle shredded cheddar cheese and grated Parmesan cheese over the entire pizza.
    - Season with salt and pepper to taste.
6. **Bake the Pizza:**
    - Transfer the pizza (on the parchment paper) onto the preheated pizza stone or baking sheet in the oven.
    - Bake for 10-12 minutes, or until the crust is golden brown and the cheese is bubbly and melted.
7. **Finish and Serve:**
    - Remove the pizza from the oven and let it cool slightly.

- Garnish with chopped fresh parsley or basil.
- Optionally, sprinkle with red pepper flakes for a bit of heat.
8. **Slice and Enjoy:**
   - Slice the breakfast pizza into wedges and serve hot.

**Tips:**

- Customize your breakfast pizza with additional toppings such as sliced tomatoes, bell peppers, onions, or mushrooms.
- For a creamier texture, you can add dollops of ricotta cheese or small pieces of fresh mozzarella.
- Serve with a side of hot sauce or salsa for extra flavor.

This breakfast pizza with eggs and bacon is a delicious and hearty meal that's perfect for brunch or even dinner. Enjoy the combination of savory toppings and gooey cheese on a crispy pizza crust!

# Overnight Oats with Berries and Honey

## Ingredients:

- 1/2 cup old-fashioned rolled oats
- 1/2 cup milk (dairy milk, almond milk, soy milk, etc.)
- 1/2 cup Greek yogurt
- 1 tablespoon chia seeds (optional, for added thickness)
- 1/2 cup mixed berries (such as strawberries, blueberries, raspberries)
- 1-2 tablespoons honey (adjust to taste)
- 1/2 teaspoon vanilla extract
- Pinch of salt

## Instructions:

1. **Combine Ingredients:**
   In a mason jar or airtight container, combine the rolled oats, milk, Greek yogurt, chia seeds (if using), vanilla extract, and a pinch of salt. Stir well to combine.
2. **Add Berries and Honey:**
   Gently fold in the mixed berries into the oat mixture. You can use fresh berries or frozen berries (thawed and drained).
3. **Sweeten with Honey:**
   Drizzle honey over the oat mixture according to your taste preferences. Stir again to distribute the honey evenly.
4. **Refrigerate Overnight:**
   Cover the jar or container with a lid and refrigerate overnight, or for at least 4 hours. This allows the oats to absorb the liquid and soften.
5. **Serve:**
   The next morning, give the overnight oats a good stir. If the mixture is too thick, you can add a splash of milk to loosen it to your desired consistency.
6. **Optional Toppings:**
   Before serving, you can top the overnight oats with additional fresh berries, a drizzle of honey, a sprinkle of granola, or a dollop of yogurt for extra flavor and texture.

## Tips:

- Use a ratio of 1:1:1 for oats, milk/yogurt, and fruit to create a balanced overnight oats base.
- Adjust the sweetness by adding more or less honey, or substitute with maple syrup or agave syrup.
- Overnight oats can be stored in the refrigerator for up to 3 days. Make a batch ahead of time for quick and healthy breakfasts throughout the week.
- Experiment with different combinations of fruits and toppings to create your favorite flavor variations.

Enjoy this nutritious and easy-to-prepare breakfast of overnight oats with berries and honey, perfect for a refreshing start to your day!

# Sausage and Egg Breakfast Casserole

## Ingredients:

- 1 lb breakfast sausage (pork or turkey), casings removed
- 6 slices bread (white, whole wheat, or sourdough), cubed
- 2 cups shredded cheddar cheese (or cheese of your choice)
- 6 large eggs
- 2 cups milk
- 1 teaspoon Dijon mustard
- 1/2 teaspoon salt
- 1/4 teaspoon black pepper
- 1/4 teaspoon garlic powder
- Optional: chopped green onions or parsley for garnish

## Instructions:

1. **Preheat the Oven:**
   Preheat your oven to 350°F (175°C). Grease a 9x13-inch baking dish with butter or cooking spray.
2. **Cook the Sausage:**
   In a large skillet, cook the breakfast sausage over medium-high heat, breaking it apart with a spoon, until browned and cooked through. Drain excess fat if necessary.
3. **Prepare the Bread and Cheese:**
   Spread half of the cubed bread in an even layer in the prepared baking dish. Top with half of the cooked sausage and half of the shredded cheese. Repeat with the remaining bread, sausage, and cheese.
4. **Whisk the Eggs and Milk Mixture:**
   In a large bowl, whisk together the eggs, milk, Dijon mustard, salt, pepper, and garlic powder until well combined.
5. **Pour Egg Mixture Over:**
   Slowly pour the egg mixture evenly over the bread, sausage, and cheese layers in the baking dish. Press down gently with a spatula to ensure all the bread cubes are submerged in the egg mixture.
6. **Bake:**
   Bake the casserole in the preheated oven for 45-55 minutes, or until the top is golden brown and the center is set. To check for doneness, insert a knife in the center – it should come out clean.
7. **Cool and Serve:**
   Remove from the oven and let the casserole cool for a few minutes before serving. Garnish with chopped green onions or parsley if desired.
8. **Serve Warm:**
   Slice the casserole into squares and serve warm. It's delicious on its own or served with a side of fresh fruit or a green salad.

**Tips:**

- You can prepare this breakfast casserole the night before. Simply assemble everything as instructed, cover with plastic wrap, and refrigerate overnight. Bake it in the morning for a quick and hearty breakfast.
- Customize the casserole by adding diced bell peppers, onions, mushrooms, or spinach for extra flavor and nutrition.
- Leftovers can be stored covered in the refrigerator for up to 3 days. Reheat in the microwave or oven until warmed through before serving.

This sausage and egg breakfast casserole is a crowd-pleasing dish that's perfect for feeding a family or serving at brunch gatherings. Enjoy the hearty flavors and comforting textures in every bite!

## Strawberry Banana Smoothie Bowl

**Ingredients:**

- 1 ripe banana, frozen
- 1 cup frozen strawberries
- 1/2 cup plain Greek yogurt
- 1/4 cup milk (dairy or non-dairy, as preferred)
- 1 tablespoon honey or maple syrup (optional, for added sweetness)
- Toppings (optional): sliced fresh strawberries, sliced banana, granola, chia seeds, shredded coconut, nuts, honey drizzle

**Instructions:**

1. **Prepare the Smoothie Base:**
    - In a blender, combine the frozen banana, frozen strawberries, Greek yogurt, milk, and honey or maple syrup (if using). Blend until smooth and creamy. Add more milk as needed to achieve your desired consistency.
2. **Assemble the Smoothie Bowl:**
    - Pour the smoothie mixture into a bowl.
3. **Add Toppings:**
    - Arrange sliced fresh strawberries, sliced banana, granola, chia seeds, shredded coconut, nuts, or any other toppings of your choice over the smoothie bowl.
4. **Serve:**
    - Serve the strawberry banana smoothie bowl immediately and enjoy it with a spoon!

**Tips:**

- For a thicker smoothie bowl, use less milk or add more frozen fruits.
- Customize your smoothie bowl with additional toppings such as berries, seeds, or nuts for added texture and nutrition.
- You can adjust the sweetness by adding more honey or maple syrup, depending on your taste preference.
- Feel free to experiment with different combinations of fruits and toppings to create your own unique smoothie bowl.

This strawberry banana smoothie bowl is not only delicious but also packed with vitamins, minerals, and antioxidants from the fruits and toppings, making it a healthy and satisfying breakfast or snack option. Enjoy the vibrant flavors and textures in every spoonful!

**Corned Beef Hash with Fried Eggs**

**Ingredients:**

- 2 cups cooked corned beef, diced (leftover from a previous meal or canned)
- 2 cups potatoes, peeled and diced (about 2 medium potatoes)
- 1 onion, finely chopped
- 1 red bell pepper, diced
- 2 cloves garlic, minced
- 2 tablespoons olive oil or butter
- Salt and pepper, to taste
- 4 eggs
- Fresh parsley or green onions, chopped (for garnish, optional)

**Instructions:**

1. **Prepare the Potatoes:**
    - If using raw potatoes, boil or steam the diced potatoes until they are just tender but not mushy. Drain and set aside.
2. **Cook the Vegetables:**
    - In a large skillet, heat olive oil or melt butter over medium heat. Add chopped onion and diced red bell pepper. Cook until softened, about 5-7 minutes.
3. **Add Corned Beef and Potatoes:**
    - Add the diced corned beef and cooked potatoes to the skillet. Stir well to combine with the vegetables. Season with salt and pepper to taste.
4. **Cook Until Crispy:**
    - Spread the mixture evenly in the skillet and let it cook undisturbed for a few minutes to develop a crispy crust on the bottom. Stir occasionally to ensure even browning. Cook for about 10-15 minutes, or until the hash is crispy and golden brown.
5. **Fry the Eggs:**
    - While the hash is cooking, fry the eggs in a separate skillet or in batches, depending on the size of your skillet. Heat a little oil or butter over medium heat, crack the eggs into the skillet, and cook until the whites are set and the yolks are still runny, or to your desired doneness.
6. **Serve:**
    - Divide the corned beef hash among plates or bowls. Top each serving with a fried egg.
    - Garnish with chopped fresh parsley or green onions if desired.
7. **Enjoy:**
    - Serve the corned beef hash with fried eggs immediately, while hot. You can also serve it with toast or a side of greens for a complete meal.

**Tips:**

- For extra flavor, you can add Worcestershire sauce or hot sauce to the corned beef hash while cooking.
- Make sure to spread out the hash evenly in the skillet and resist the urge to stir too frequently to allow it to develop a crispy texture.
- Leftover corned beef hash can be stored in an airtight container in the refrigerator for up to 3 days. Reheat gently on the stove or in the microwave before serving.

This corned beef hash with fried eggs recipe is a comforting and satisfying dish that's perfect for a leisurely weekend breakfast or brunch. Enjoy the delicious blend of flavors and textures in every bite!

**Breakfast Croissant with Ham and Swiss**

**Ingredients:**

- 2 large croissants
- 4 slices of ham (thinly sliced)
- 4 slices of Swiss cheese
- 2 large eggs
- 2 tablespoons butter
- Salt and pepper, to taste
- Optional: Dijon mustard, mayonnaise, or honey mustard for spreading

**Instructions:**

1. **Prepare the Croissants:**
   Preheat your oven to 350°F (175°C). Slice the croissants in half horizontally, creating a top and bottom half.
2. **Assemble the Croissants:**
   - If desired, spread Dijon mustard, mayonnaise, or honey mustard on the bottom halves of the croissants.
   - Layer each bottom half with 2 slices of ham and 2 slices of Swiss cheese.
3. **Prepare the Eggs:**
   - In a skillet, melt 1 tablespoon of butter over medium heat.
   - Crack the eggs into the skillet and cook to your desired doneness (fried, scrambled, or poached). Season with salt and pepper.
4. **Assemble and Bake:**
   - Place the cooked eggs on top of the Swiss cheese slices on each croissant.
   - Place the top halves of the croissants over the eggs to form sandwiches.
5. **Bake:**
   - Transfer the assembled croissants to a baking sheet lined with parchment paper.
   - Bake in the preheated oven for about 5-7 minutes, or until the croissants are warmed through and the cheese is melted.
6. **Serve:**
   - Remove from the oven and serve the breakfast croissants warm.

**Tips:**

- You can customize your breakfast croissant with additional ingredients such as sliced tomatoes, avocado, or spinach.
- If you prefer a more toasted croissant, you can toast the halves before assembling the sandwiches.
- For a quicker option, you can skip baking and serve the croissants immediately after assembling.

This breakfast croissant with ham and Swiss cheese is a delicious way to start your day with its buttery croissant, savory ham, melted Swiss cheese, and a perfectly cooked egg. Enjoy this indulgent treat for breakfast or brunch!

**Pumpkin Pancakes with Whipped Cream**

**Ingredients:**

For the Pumpkin Pancakes:

- 1 cup all-purpose flour
- 1 tablespoon granulated sugar
- 1 teaspoon baking powder
- 1/2 teaspoon baking soda
- 1/2 teaspoon salt
- 1 teaspoon ground cinnamon
- 1/2 teaspoon ground nutmeg
- 1/4 teaspoon ground ginger
- 1/4 teaspoon ground cloves
- 1/2 cup pumpkin puree
- 1 cup buttermilk (or substitute with milk mixed with 1 tablespoon vinegar or lemon juice)
- 1 large egg
- 2 tablespoons unsalted butter, melted
- 1 teaspoon vanilla extract

For the Whipped Cream:

- 1 cup heavy cream, chilled
- 2 tablespoons powdered sugar
- 1/2 teaspoon vanilla extract

**Instructions:**

1. **Prepare the Whipped Cream:**
   - In a large mixing bowl, combine the chilled heavy cream, powdered sugar, and vanilla extract.
   - Using a hand mixer or stand mixer with the whisk attachment, beat the mixture on medium-high speed until stiff peaks form. Be careful not to overmix. Set aside or refrigerate until ready to use.
2. **Make the Pumpkin Pancakes:**
   - In a large bowl, whisk together the flour, sugar, baking powder, baking soda, salt, cinnamon, nutmeg, ginger, and cloves.
   - In another bowl, whisk together the pumpkin puree, buttermilk, egg, melted butter, and vanilla extract until smooth.
   - Pour the wet ingredients into the dry ingredients and stir until just combined. It's okay if the batter is slightly lumpy.
   - Let the batter rest for 5-10 minutes while you preheat a griddle or non-stick skillet over medium heat. Lightly grease the griddle or skillet with butter or cooking spray.

3. **Cook the Pancakes:**
   - Pour about 1/4 cup of batter onto the hot griddle for each pancake. Cook until bubbles form on the surface of the pancakes and the edges look set, about 2-3 minutes.
   - Flip the pancakes and cook on the other side until golden brown, about 1-2 minutes more.
   - Transfer the cooked pancakes to a plate and keep them warm while you cook the remaining batter.
4. **Serve:**
   - Stack the pumpkin pancakes on serving plates.
   - Top each stack with a generous dollop of whipped cream.
5. **Optional Garnish:**
   - Sprinkle with a dash of cinnamon or nutmeg, and optionally drizzle with maple syrup or honey.
6. **Enjoy:**
   - Serve the pumpkin pancakes with whipped cream immediately while warm.

**Tips:**

- To keep pancakes warm while cooking the rest, place them on a baking sheet in a 200°F (93°C) oven.
- For extra pumpkin flavor, you can add a tablespoon of pumpkin pie spice to the pancake batter.
- If you prefer a lighter topping, you can use store-bought whipped cream instead of making your own.

These pumpkin pancakes with whipped cream are a delightful and indulgent treat, perfect for enjoying during the fall season or any time you're craving something comforting and delicious for breakfast!

**Breakfast Enchiladas with Salsa Verde**

**Ingredients:**

For the Enchiladas:

- 8 small flour tortillas
- 1 cup cooked and shredded chicken or cooked breakfast sausage (optional)
- 1 cup shredded Monterey Jack cheese or Mexican cheese blend
- 4 large eggs
- 1/2 cup milk
- Salt and pepper, to taste
- 1 tablespoon butter or olive oil
- Optional: chopped cilantro or green onions for garnish

For the Salsa Verde:

- 1 pound tomatillos, husked and rinsed
- 1/2 onion, chopped
- 2 cloves garlic, minced
- 1 jalapeño pepper, seeded and chopped (optional, adjust to taste)
- 1/2 cup chopped fresh cilantro
- Juice of 1 lime
- Salt and pepper, to taste

**Instructions:**

1. **Prepare the Salsa Verde:**
   - In a medium saucepan, combine the tomatillos, chopped onion, minced garlic, and jalapeño (if using). Cover with water and bring to a boil over medium-high heat.
   - Reduce heat and simmer for about 10-15 minutes, until the tomatillos are soft and cooked through.
   - Drain the tomatillos and transfer them to a blender. Add chopped cilantro, lime juice, salt, and pepper. Blend until smooth. Set aside.
2. **Prepare the Enchiladas:**
   - Preheat your oven to 375°F (190°C). Grease a 9x13-inch baking dish with butter or cooking spray.
   - In a large skillet, heat butter or olive oil over medium heat. Add eggs, milk, salt, and pepper. Scramble the eggs until they are just set. Remove from heat and set aside.
3. **Assemble the Enchiladas:**
   - Warm the flour tortillas slightly to make them pliable (you can do this in the microwave for a few seconds or on a dry skillet).

- Divide the scrambled eggs evenly among the tortillas, placing a portion along the center of each tortilla. Add a sprinkle of shredded chicken or breakfast sausage (if using).
- Roll up each tortilla and place seam-side down in the prepared baking dish.

4. **Pour Salsa Verde Over Enchiladas:**
   - Pour the salsa verde evenly over the assembled enchiladas in the baking dish, covering them completely.

5. **Bake:**
   - Sprinkle shredded cheese over the top of the enchiladas.
   - Cover the baking dish with foil and bake in the preheated oven for 20 minutes.
   - Remove the foil and bake for an additional 5-10 minutes, until the cheese is melted and bubbly.

6. **Serve:**
   - Remove from the oven and let the enchiladas cool slightly before serving.
   - Garnish with chopped cilantro or green onions if desired.
   - Serve the breakfast enchiladas with salsa verde warm, and enjoy!

**Tips:**

- You can prepare the salsa verde ahead of time and store it in the refrigerator for up to a week.
- Customize the filling by adding black beans, diced tomatoes, or bell peppers.
- Serve with sour cream, avocado slices, or a side of refried beans for a complete meal.

These breakfast enchiladas with salsa verde are flavorful, comforting, and perfect for a weekend brunch or special breakfast. Enjoy the delicious blend of eggs, cheese, and salsa verde wrapped in warm tortillas!

**Blueberry Scones**

**Ingredients:**

- 2 cups all-purpose flour
- 1/3 cup granulated sugar
- 1 tablespoon baking powder
- 1/2 teaspoon salt
- 1/2 cup unsalted butter, cold and cut into small pieces
- 1 cup fresh or frozen blueberries
- 1/2 cup milk (plus more for brushing)
- 1 large egg
- 1 teaspoon vanilla extract
- Optional: coarse sugar for sprinkling on top

**Instructions:**

1. **Preheat the Oven:**
   Preheat your oven to 400°F (200°C). Line a baking sheet with parchment paper or silicone mat.
2. **Prepare Dry Ingredients:**
   In a large bowl, whisk together the flour, sugar, baking powder, and salt.
3. **Cut in Butter:**
   Add the cold butter pieces to the dry ingredients. Use a pastry cutter or your fingertips to quickly work the butter into the flour mixture until it resembles coarse crumbs. Some larger pea-sized pieces of butter are okay.
4. **Add Blueberries:**
   Gently fold the blueberries into the flour mixture, being careful not to crush them.
5. **Mix Wet Ingredients:**
   In a separate bowl, whisk together the milk, egg, and vanilla extract.
6. **Combine and Form Dough:**
   Pour the wet ingredients into the dry ingredients. Stir gently with a spatula or wooden spoon until the dough starts to come together. It will be slightly sticky.
7. **Shape Scones:**
   Turn the dough out onto a lightly floured surface. Pat it into a 1-inch thick circle. Cut the circle into 8 wedges.
8. **Bake:**
   Place the scones on the prepared baking sheet, spacing them a few inches apart. Brush the tops with a little milk and sprinkle with coarse sugar if desired.
9. **Bake:**
   Bake in the preheated oven for 15-18 minutes, or until the scones are golden brown on top and cooked through.
10. **Cool and Serve:**

Transfer the scones to a wire rack to cool slightly before serving. Enjoy warm or at room temperature.

**Tips:**

- If using frozen blueberries, you can toss them with a tablespoon of flour before adding them to the dough. This helps prevent them from bleeding into the dough.
- Handle the dough gently to ensure tender scones. Overmixing or handling the dough too much can result in tough scones.
- Serve the blueberry scones with clotted cream, butter, or your favorite jam for a delightful treat.

These homemade blueberry scones are buttery, tender, and bursting with juicy blueberries. They are perfect for enjoying fresh out of the oven with a cup of tea or coffee. Enjoy baking and savoring these delicious treats!

## Quinoa Breakfast Bowl with Spinach and Egg

**Ingredients:**

- 1 cup quinoa, rinsed
- 2 cups water or vegetable broth
- 1 tablespoon olive oil
- 2 cups fresh spinach leaves
- 2 cloves garlic, minced
- Salt and pepper, to taste
- 4 large eggs
- Optional toppings: sliced avocado, cherry tomatoes, feta cheese, hot sauce

**Instructions:**

1. **Cook Quinoa:**
   - In a medium saucepan, combine quinoa and water or vegetable broth. Bring to a boil over high heat.
   - Reduce heat to low, cover, and simmer for about 15 minutes, or until quinoa is tender and liquid is absorbed. Remove from heat and let it sit covered for 5 minutes. Fluff with a fork.
2. **Prepare Spinach:**
   - In a large skillet, heat olive oil over medium heat. Add minced garlic and cook for about 1 minute until fragrant.
   - Add fresh spinach leaves to the skillet. Cook, stirring occasionally, until spinach is wilted. Season with salt and pepper to taste.
3. **Cook Eggs:**
   - While the spinach is cooking, fry or poach the eggs according to your preference in another skillet.
4. **Assemble Breakfast Bowls:**
   - Divide the cooked quinoa evenly among serving bowls.
   - Top each bowl with sautéed spinach.
   - Place a fried or poached egg on top of the spinach.
5. **Add Optional Toppings:**
   - Garnish each bowl with sliced avocado, cherry tomatoes, crumbled feta cheese, and a drizzle of hot sauce if desired.
6. **Serve:**
   - Serve the quinoa breakfast bowls immediately, while the eggs are still warm.

**Tips:**

- You can prepare the quinoa and spinach ahead of time and reheat them when ready to assemble the bowls.
- Customize your breakfast bowl with additional toppings such as chopped herbs, diced bell peppers, or a sprinkle of seeds.

- For extra flavor, you can add a dash of soy sauce or a squeeze of lemon juice to the spinach while cooking.

This quinoa breakfast bowl with spinach and egg is packed with protein, fiber, and essential nutrients, making it a healthy and satisfying choice to start your day. Enjoy the delicious combination of flavors and textures in each bite!

**Cinnamon Sugar Donuts**

**Ingredients:**

For the donuts:

- 1 cup all-purpose flour
- 1 teaspoon baking powder
- 1/4 teaspoon baking soda
- 1/4 teaspoon salt
- 1/2 teaspoon ground cinnamon
- 1/3 cup granulated sugar
- 1/4 cup milk
- 1/4 cup plain yogurt or sour cream
- 1 large egg
- 2 tablespoons unsalted butter, melted
- 1 teaspoon vanilla extract

For the cinnamon sugar coating:

- 1/2 cup granulated sugar
- 1 teaspoon ground cinnamon
- 4 tablespoons unsalted butter, melted (for dipping)

**Instructions:**

1. **Preheat the Oven:**
   Preheat your oven to 350°F (175°C). Grease a donut pan with butter or cooking spray.
2. **Prepare the Donut Batter:**
   - In a large bowl, whisk together the flour, baking powder, baking soda, salt, cinnamon, and granulated sugar.
   - In another bowl, whisk together the milk, yogurt or sour cream, egg, melted butter, and vanilla extract until smooth.
   - Pour the wet ingredients into the dry ingredients and stir until just combined. Do not overmix.
3. **Fill the Donut Pan:**
   - Spoon or pipe the batter into the prepared donut pan, filling each mold about 2/3 full.
4. **Bake:**
   - Bake in the preheated oven for 10-12 minutes, or until the donuts spring back when lightly touched and a toothpick inserted into the center comes out clean.
5. **Prepare the Cinnamon Sugar Coating:**
   - In a shallow bowl, mix together the granulated sugar and ground cinnamon for the coating.
6. **Coat the Donuts:**

- While the donuts are still warm, carefully remove them from the pan.
- Dip each donut in the melted butter, coating both sides.
- Immediately dip the buttered donut into the cinnamon sugar mixture, rolling it around to coat evenly.

7. **Serve:**
   - Place the cinnamon sugar-coated donuts on a wire rack to cool slightly before serving.

**Tips:**

- If you don't have a donut pan, you can use a mini muffin tin to make donut holes.
- These donuts are best enjoyed fresh on the day they are made, but you can store leftovers in an airtight container at room temperature for up to 2 days.
- For a richer flavor, you can add a pinch of ground nutmeg or cloves to the cinnamon sugar mixture.

Enjoy these homemade cinnamon sugar donuts with a cup of coffee or tea for a delightful treat that's perfect for breakfast or snack time!

## Breakfast BLT (Bacon, Lettuce, Tomato) Sandwich

### Ingredients:

- 4 slices of bread (toasted, if desired)
- 8 slices of bacon
- 1 large tomato, sliced
- 1 cup lettuce leaves (such as romaine or leaf lettuce)
- 4 eggs
- Salt and pepper, to taste
- Mayonnaise or aioli, to taste
- Optional: sliced avocado, cheese slices (cheddar or Swiss)

### Instructions:

1. **Cook Bacon:**
   - In a skillet over medium heat, cook the bacon until crispy, turning occasionally. Remove from the skillet and drain on paper towels.
2. **Cook Eggs:**
   - In the same skillet, cook the eggs to your preference (fried, scrambled, or poached). Season with salt and pepper.
3. **Assemble the Sandwich:**
   - Spread mayonnaise or aioli on one side of each slice of bread.
   - Layer lettuce leaves on the bottom slice of bread.
   - Arrange sliced tomato on top of the lettuce.
   - Place cooked bacon slices over the tomato.
   - Add the cooked eggs on top of the bacon.
   - If desired, add sliced avocado or cheese slices on top of the eggs.
   - Top with the remaining slice of bread, mayo side down.
4. **Serve:**
   - Cut the sandwich in half diagonally, if desired, and serve immediately.

### Tips:

- You can customize your Breakfast BLT Sandwich by adding extras like sliced avocado, cheese, or a drizzle of hot sauce.
- Use good quality, thick-cut bacon for the best flavor and texture.
- Toasting the bread adds extra crunch to the sandwich, but it's optional depending on your preference.
- For a healthier option, you can use whole grain or multi-grain bread instead of white bread.

This Breakfast BLT Sandwich is a satisfying and flavorful way to start your day, combining crispy bacon, fresh vegetables, eggs, and creamy mayo for a delicious breakfast treat. Enjoy it with a side of fruit or a cup of coffee for a complete meal!

# Breakfast Bread Pudding with Berries

## Ingredients:

- 6 cups cubed bread (such as French bread or brioche), preferably stale or day-old
- 1 cup mixed berries (such as blueberries, raspberries, and strawberries), fresh or frozen
- 4 large eggs
- 1 1/2 cups milk (whole milk or any milk of your choice)
- 1/2 cup heavy cream
- 1/2 cup granulated sugar
- 1 teaspoon vanilla extract
- 1/2 teaspoon ground cinnamon
- 1/4 teaspoon ground nutmeg
- Pinch of salt
- 2 tablespoons unsalted butter, melted

## Optional Toppings:

- Powdered sugar, for dusting
- Maple syrup or honey, for drizzling
- Whipped cream or yogurt, for serving

## Instructions:

1. **Preheat the Oven:**
   Preheat your oven to 350°F (175°C). Grease a 9x13-inch baking dish with butter or cooking spray.
2. **Prepare the Bread and Berries:**
   - Spread the cubed bread evenly in the prepared baking dish. Sprinkle the mixed berries over the bread cubes.
3. **Prepare the Custard Mixture:**
   - In a large bowl, whisk together the eggs, milk, heavy cream, granulated sugar, vanilla extract, cinnamon, nutmeg, and a pinch of salt until well combined.
4. **Assemble the Bread Pudding:**
   - Pour the custard mixture evenly over the bread cubes and berries in the baking dish. Press down lightly with a spoon or spatula to ensure all the bread cubes are soaked in the custard.
5. **Let it Sit:**
   - Let the bread pudding mixture sit for about 15-20 minutes to allow the bread to absorb the custard.
6. **Bake:**
   - Drizzle the melted butter evenly over the top of the bread pudding.
   - Bake in the preheated oven for 40-45 minutes, or until the top is golden brown and the custard is set.
7. **Serve:**

- Remove from the oven and let the bread pudding cool slightly before serving.
- Dust with powdered sugar, if desired, and serve warm with maple syrup, honey, whipped cream, or yogurt on the side.

**Tips:**

- You can use any type of bread you have on hand, but crusty bread like French bread or brioche works particularly well for bread pudding.
- If using frozen berries, you can thaw them slightly and pat them dry with paper towels before adding to the bread cubes.
- Leftover bread pudding can be stored in an airtight container in the refrigerator for up to 3 days. Reheat gently in the microwave or oven before serving.

This breakfast bread pudding with berries is a delightful combination of soft, custardy bread and juicy berries, making it a perfect sweet treat for breakfast or brunch. Enjoy the warm flavors and comforting texture of this delicious dish!

## Sweet Potato Hash with Poached Eggs

### Ingredients:

- 2 medium sweet potatoes, peeled and diced into small cubes
- 1 bell pepper, diced (any color)
- 1 small onion, diced
- 2 cloves garlic, minced
- 2 tablespoons olive oil
- 1 teaspoon smoked paprika
- 1/2 teaspoon ground cumin
- Salt and pepper, to taste
- 4 large eggs
- Optional toppings: chopped fresh herbs (such as parsley or chives), hot sauce, avocado slices

### Instructions:

1. **Prepare the Sweet Potato Hash:**
   - Heat olive oil in a large skillet over medium heat.
   - Add diced sweet potatoes to the skillet and cook, stirring occasionally, for about 8-10 minutes or until they start to soften and brown slightly.
2. **Add Vegetables and Seasonings:**
   - Add diced bell pepper, onion, and minced garlic to the skillet with the sweet potatoes.
   - Season with smoked paprika, ground cumin, salt, and pepper.
   - Continue cooking, stirring occasionally, for another 5-7 minutes or until the vegetables are tender and the sweet potatoes are cooked through.
3. **Poach the Eggs:**
   - While the hash is cooking, poach the eggs. Bring a medium pot of water to a simmer over medium heat.
   - Crack each egg into a small bowl or ramekin. Create a gentle whirlpool in the simmering water with a spoon and carefully slide the egg into the center of the whirlpool. Repeat for each egg.
   - Cook the eggs for about 3-4 minutes for a runny yolk or longer for a firmer yolk. Remove the poached eggs with a slotted spoon and drain on a paper towel.
4. **Serve:**
   - Divide the sweet potato hash among serving plates.
   - Top each serving with a poached egg.
   - Garnish with chopped fresh herbs, hot sauce, and avocado slices if desired.

### Tips:

- To save time, you can microwave diced sweet potatoes for a few minutes before adding them to the skillet to speed up the cooking process.

- Customize your sweet potato hash by adding other vegetables like spinach, mushrooms, or cherry tomatoes.
- For a creamier texture, you can top the sweet potato hash with a dollop of Greek yogurt or sour cream.

This sweet potato hash with poached eggs is a satisfying and nutritious breakfast that's packed with flavor and wholesome ingredients. Enjoy this delicious dish to start your day right!

**Cranberry Orange Muffins**

**Ingredients:**

- 2 cups all-purpose flour
- 3/4 cup granulated sugar
- 1 tablespoon baking powder
- 1/2 teaspoon baking soda
- 1/2 teaspoon salt
- 1 cup fresh or frozen cranberries, chopped
- Zest of 1 orange
- 1/2 cup unsalted butter, melted and cooled
- 3/4 cup fresh orange juice (about 2 oranges)
- 2 large eggs
- 1 teaspoon vanilla extract

**For the optional glaze:**

- 1 cup powdered sugar
- 2-3 tablespoons fresh orange juice

**Instructions:**

1. **Preheat the Oven:**
   Preheat your oven to 375°F (190°C). Line a 12-cup muffin tin with paper liners or grease the muffin cups.
2. **Prepare the Dry Ingredients:**
   In a large bowl, whisk together the flour, sugar, baking powder, baking soda, and salt.
3. **Prepare the Wet Ingredients:**
   In another bowl, whisk together the melted butter, orange juice, eggs, and vanilla extract until well combined.
4. **Combine Wet and Dry Ingredients:**
   Pour the wet ingredients into the dry ingredients and stir gently with a spatula or wooden spoon until just combined. Do not overmix.
5. **Fold in Cranberries and Orange Zest:**
   Gently fold in the chopped cranberries and orange zest into the batter.
6. **Fill Muffin Cups:**
   Divide the batter evenly among the prepared muffin cups, filling each cup almost to the top.
7. **Bake:**
   Bake in the preheated oven for 18-20 minutes, or until the muffins are golden brown and a toothpick inserted into the center comes out clean.
8. **Cool:**
   Allow the muffins to cool in the pan for 5 minutes, then transfer them to a wire rack to cool completely.

9. **Optional Glaze:**
    - If desired, whisk together powdered sugar and orange juice in a small bowl to make a glaze.
    - Drizzle the glaze over the cooled muffins.
10. **Serve:**
Serve the cranberry orange muffins warm or at room temperature. Enjoy!

**Tips:**

- If using frozen cranberries, do not thaw them before chopping and folding into the batter.
- For extra citrus flavor, you can add a tablespoon of orange zest to the glaze mixture.
- Store leftover muffins in an airtight container at room temperature for up to 3 days, or freeze for longer storage.

These cranberry orange muffins are moist, flavorful, and perfect for breakfast or as a snack. The combination of tart cranberries and fresh orange zest makes them a delightful treat any time of year!

# Breakfast Strata with Ham and Cheese

## Ingredients:

- 8 slices of bread, preferably day-old, cut into cubes
- 1 cup cooked ham, diced
- 1 cup shredded cheese (such as cheddar, Swiss, or Gruyère)
- 6 large eggs
- 2 cups milk
- 1/2 teaspoon salt
- 1/4 teaspoon black pepper
- 1/2 teaspoon mustard powder (optional)
- 1/4 cup chopped fresh parsley or chives (optional, for garnish)

## Instructions:

1. **Prepare the Bread and Ham:**
   - Grease a 9x13-inch baking dish with butter or cooking spray. Spread the cubed bread evenly in the baking dish. Sprinkle diced ham and shredded cheese over the bread cubes.
2. **Prepare the Egg Mixture:**
   - In a large bowl, whisk together eggs, milk, salt, pepper, and mustard powder (if using) until well combined.
3. **Assemble the Strata:**
   - Pour the egg mixture evenly over the bread, ham, and cheese in the baking dish. Press down lightly with a spoon or spatula to ensure all the bread cubes are soaked in the egg mixture.
   - Cover the baking dish with plastic wrap and refrigerate for at least 2 hours or overnight. This allows the bread to absorb the egg mixture.
4. **Bake the Strata:**
   - Preheat your oven to 350°F (175°C). Remove the strata from the refrigerator and let it sit at room temperature while the oven preheats.
   - Bake uncovered for 45-50 minutes, or until the top is golden brown and the egg mixture is set. To check for doneness, insert a knife into the center of the strata – if it comes out clean, it's ready.
5. **Serve:**
   - Remove from the oven and let the strata cool for a few minutes before slicing and serving.
   - Garnish with chopped fresh parsley or chives if desired.

## Tips:

- You can customize your breakfast strata by adding other ingredients like sautéed vegetables (such as spinach or bell peppers), cooked bacon, or different types of cheese.

- Make sure to use day-old bread or slightly stale bread for the best texture, as it will absorb the egg mixture better without becoming mushy.
- Leftover strata can be stored in the refrigerator for up to 3 days. Reheat individual portions in the microwave or oven before serving.

This breakfast strata with ham and cheese is a hearty and satisfying dish that's perfect for feeding a crowd or enjoying as leftovers throughout the week. It's easy to prepare ahead of time and always a hit at brunch gatherings!

**Nutella Stuffed French Toast**

**Ingredients:**

- 8 slices of bread (thick-cut preferred, such as brioche or challah)
- Nutella or chocolate hazelnut spread
- 4 large eggs
- 1/2 cup milk
- 1 teaspoon vanilla extract
- 1/2 teaspoon ground cinnamon
- Pinch of salt
- Butter or cooking spray, for cooking
- Powdered sugar, for dusting (optional)
- Fresh berries or banana slices, for serving (optional)

**Instructions:**

1. **Prepare the Bread:**
   - Spread Nutella generously on 4 slices of bread. Place the remaining 4 slices of bread on top to make 4 Nutella sandwiches.
2. **Prepare the Egg Mixture:**
   - In a shallow dish or bowl, whisk together eggs, milk, vanilla extract, cinnamon, and a pinch of salt until well combined.
3. **Dip and Coat:**
   - Heat a large skillet or griddle over medium heat and melt a pat of butter or spray with cooking spray.
   - Dip each Nutella sandwich into the egg mixture, coating both sides evenly.
4. **Cook the French Toast:**
   - Place the dipped sandwiches on the skillet or griddle. Cook for about 3-4 minutes on each side, or until golden brown and crispy.
   - Repeat with the remaining sandwiches, adding more butter or cooking spray as needed.
5. **Serve:**
   - Remove the Nutella stuffed French toast from the skillet and place on serving plates.
   - Dust with powdered sugar if desired.
   - Serve warm with fresh berries or banana slices on the side.

**Tips:**

- Ensure that the Nutella sandwiches are sealed well around the edges to prevent the Nutella from oozing out during cooking.
- You can customize your stuffed French toast by adding sliced bananas or strawberries inside the sandwiches along with the Nutella.

- For an extra indulgence, serve with a dollop of whipped cream or a drizzle of maple syrup.

This Nutella stuffed French toast is sure to be a hit at breakfast or brunch, combining the rich flavors of Nutella with the comforting warmth of French toast. Enjoy this decadent treat with your favorite toppings and a hot cup of coffee or tea!

# Breakfast Crepes with Fresh Fruit

**Ingredients:**

For the crepes:

- 1 cup all-purpose flour
- 2 large eggs
- 1 cup milk
- 1/4 cup water
- 2 tablespoons unsalted butter, melted
- 1 tablespoon granulated sugar (optional)
- 1/2 teaspoon vanilla extract (optional)
- Pinch of salt

For the filling and topping:

- Fresh fruits such as strawberries, blueberries, raspberries, and bananas, sliced
- Whipped cream or Greek yogurt
- Honey or maple syrup, for drizzling
- Powdered sugar, for dusting (optional)
- Lemon wedges (optional, for serving)

**Instructions:**

1. **Make the Crepe Batter:**
    - In a blender or mixing bowl, combine flour, eggs, milk, water, melted butter, sugar (if using), vanilla extract (if using), and a pinch of salt. Blend or whisk until smooth. Let the batter rest in the refrigerator for at least 30 minutes (or up to overnight) to allow the bubbles to settle and the gluten to relax.
2. **Cook the Crepes:**
    - Heat a non-stick skillet or crepe pan over medium heat. Lightly grease the skillet with butter or cooking spray.
    - Pour about 1/4 cup of batter into the hot skillet, swirling it around to evenly coat the bottom in a thin layer.
    - Cook the crepe for about 1-2 minutes, or until the edges start to lift and the bottom is lightly golden. Flip and cook for another 1-2 minutes on the other side.
    - Transfer the cooked crepe to a plate and cover with a clean kitchen towel to keep warm. Repeat with the remaining batter, greasing the skillet as needed.
3. **Assemble the Crepes:**
    - Spread a thin layer of whipped cream or Greek yogurt over each crepe.
    - Arrange a variety of fresh fruit slices on one half of each crepe.
4. **Fold and Serve:**
    - Fold the crepes in half and then in half again to form triangles or roll them up.
    - Place the filled crepes on serving plates. Drizzle with honey or maple syrup.

- - Dust with powdered sugar if desired and garnish with additional fresh fruit.
  - Serve warm with lemon wedges on the side, if desired.

**Tips:**

- Be sure to spread the batter thinly in the skillet to achieve delicate and thin crepes.
- Customize your breakfast crepes by adding a sprinkle of cinnamon, a dash of nutmeg, or a squeeze of lemon juice to the batter.
- You can also add a dollop of Nutella, almond butter, or fruit preserves to the crepes for extra flavor.

Enjoy these breakfast crepes with fresh fruit as a special treat for breakfast or brunch. They're light, flavorful, and perfect for any occasion!

**Bacon and Cheese Breakfast Pizza**

**Ingredients:**

- 1 lb pizza dough (store-bought or homemade)
- 1 cup shredded mozzarella cheese
- 1 cup shredded cheddar cheese
- 6 slices of bacon, cooked until crispy and chopped
- 4 large eggs
- Salt and pepper, to taste
- 1 tablespoon olive oil
- Fresh parsley or chives, chopped (optional, for garnish)

**Instructions:**

1. **Preheat the Oven:**
   Preheat your oven to 450°F (230°C). Place a pizza stone or an upside-down baking sheet in the oven to preheat as well.
2. **Prepare the Pizza Dough:**
   - On a lightly floured surface, roll out the pizza dough to your desired thickness. Transfer the rolled dough to a piece of parchment paper dusted with cornmeal or flour.
3. **Assemble the Pizza:**
   - Brush the rolled-out dough with olive oil, leaving a border around the edges for the crust.
   - Sprinkle half of the shredded mozzarella and cheddar cheese evenly over the dough.
   - Scatter the chopped bacon over the cheese.
4. **Prepare the Eggs:**
   - Create 4 wells or indentations in the cheese and bacon layer.
   - Crack an egg into each well.
   - Season the eggs with salt and pepper.
5. **Bake the Pizza:**
   - Carefully transfer the pizza (on the parchment paper) onto the preheated pizza stone or baking sheet in the oven.
   - Bake for 12-15 minutes, or until the crust is golden brown, the cheese is bubbly, and the egg whites are set.
6. **Finish and Serve:**
   - Remove the pizza from the oven and let it cool slightly.
   - Sprinkle the remaining shredded cheese over the hot pizza.
   - Garnish with chopped fresh parsley or chives, if desired.
   - Slice and serve immediately.

**Tips:**

- For a crispy crust, preheat the pizza stone or baking sheet in the oven before placing the pizza on it.
- Customize your breakfast pizza by adding thinly sliced onions, bell peppers, or mushrooms before baking.
- Feel free to experiment with different cheeses such as Monterey Jack, Gouda, or Parmesan.

This Bacon and Cheese Breakfast Pizza is a delicious and savory twist on traditional breakfast items, perfect for serving at brunch or as a weekend breakfast treat. Enjoy the combination of crispy bacon, gooey cheese, and perfectly cooked eggs on a crispy pizza crust!

## English Breakfast (Eggs, Bacon, Sausage, Beans)

**Ingredients:**

- Eggs (fried, scrambled, or poached)
- Bacon slices (preferably back bacon or streaky bacon)
- Sausage links or patties (Cumberland sausages are traditional)
- Baked beans (in tomato sauce)
- Grilled tomatoes (halved)
- Sautéed mushrooms
- Black pudding slices (optional, a type of blood sausage)
- Toast or fried bread slices
- Butter or oil for cooking
- Salt and pepper to taste

**Instructions:**

1. **Cook the Bacon and Sausages:**
    - In a large frying pan or skillet, cook the bacon slices until crispy and the sausages until browned and cooked through. You can grill or oven-bake them if you prefer.
2. **Prepare the Eggs:**
    - Depending on your preference, fry, scramble, or poach the eggs in a separate pan. For fried eggs, cook until the whites are set and the yolks are runny or cooked to your liking.
3. **Prepare the Other Components:**
    - Heat the baked beans in a saucepan until hot.
    - Grill or pan-fry the tomato halves until they are lightly charred and softened.
    - Sauté the mushrooms in a little butter or oil until they are cooked through and slightly golden.
4. **Toast or Fried Bread:**
    - Toast bread slices or fry them in a little butter until golden and crisp.
5. **Assemble and Serve:**
    - Arrange the cooked bacon, sausages, eggs, grilled tomatoes, sautéed mushrooms, and black pudding slices (if using) on a large plate.
    - Serve with a portion of baked beans and toast or fried bread slices on the side.
    - Season with salt and pepper to taste.

**Tips:**

- Keep components warm by covering with foil while you finish cooking the rest of the breakfast.
- Customize your English breakfast by adding extras like hash browns, fried potatoes, or a side of HP sauce or ketchup.

- Serve with a hot cup of tea or coffee and enjoy this hearty and satisfying meal, which is perfect for a leisurely weekend brunch or a special occasion.

This classic English breakfast is a substantial meal that combines savory flavors and textures, making it a beloved choice for breakfast enthusiasts around the world.

# Lemon Poppy Seed Pancakes

## Ingredients:

- 1 cup all-purpose flour
- 2 tablespoons granulated sugar
- 1 tablespoon poppy seeds
- 1 teaspoon baking powder
- 1/2 teaspoon baking soda
- 1/4 teaspoon salt
- 1 cup buttermilk
- 1 large egg
- Zest of 1 lemon
- 2 tablespoons fresh lemon juice
- 2 tablespoons unsalted butter, melted
- Butter or oil for cooking

## Optional Toppings:

- Fresh berries (such as blueberries or raspberries)
- Maple syrup
- Powdered sugar
- Whipped cream

## Instructions:

1. **Prepare the Dry Ingredients:**
   - In a large bowl, whisk together the flour, sugar, poppy seeds, baking powder, baking soda, and salt.
2. **Prepare the Wet Ingredients:**
   - In another bowl, whisk together the buttermilk, egg, lemon zest, lemon juice, and melted butter until well combined.
3. **Combine Wet and Dry Ingredients:**
   - Pour the wet ingredients into the dry ingredients and stir gently until just combined. Do not overmix; it's okay if there are a few lumps in the batter.
4. **Cook the Pancakes:**
   - Heat a griddle or non-stick skillet over medium heat. Lightly grease the surface with butter or oil.
   - Pour about 1/4 cup of batter onto the griddle for each pancake. Cook until bubbles form on the surface of the pancake and the edges start to set, about 2-3 minutes.
5. **Flip and Cook:**
   - Carefully flip the pancakes and cook for another 1-2 minutes, or until golden brown and cooked through.
6. **Serve:**

- Remove the pancakes from the griddle and keep warm while you cook the remaining pancakes.
- Serve the lemon poppy seed pancakes warm with your choice of toppings such as fresh berries, maple syrup, powdered sugar, or whipped cream.

**Tips:**

- For extra lemon flavor, you can add a little more lemon zest or lemon juice to the batter.
- If you don't have buttermilk, you can make a substitute by adding 1 tablespoon of lemon juice or vinegar to 1 cup of milk and letting it sit for 5 minutes before using.
- To keep pancakes warm while cooking the rest, place them on a baking sheet in a 200°F (95°C) oven.

Enjoy these lemon poppy seed pancakes for a bright and flavorful breakfast or brunch. They're perfect for adding a refreshing twist to your morning routine!

**Breakfast Biscuit Sandwich with Egg and Sausage**

**Ingredients:**

- 2 large buttermilk biscuits (store-bought or homemade)
- 2 large eggs
- 2 sausage patties or cooked sausage links
- 2 slices of cheese (cheddar, American, or your favorite)
- Butter for cooking
- Salt and pepper to taste

**Instructions:**

1. **Prepare the Biscuits:**
   - If using store-bought biscuits, bake them according to the package instructions. f making homemade biscuits, prepare and bake them ahead of time until golden brown.
2. **Cook the Sausage:**
   - Heat a skillet over medium heat. Add the sausage patties or links and cook until browned and cooked through, about 4-5 minutes per side.
3. **Cook the Eggs:**
   - In the same skillet (or another skillet), melt a little butter over medium heat.
   - Crack the eggs into the skillet and cook until the whites are set and the yolks are cooked to your liking. Season with salt and pepper.
4. **Assemble the Sandwiches:**
   - Slice the biscuits in half horizontally.
   - Place a slice of cheese on the bottom half of each biscuit.
   - Top with a cooked sausage patty or sausage links.
   - Add a cooked egg on top of the sausage.
   - Place the top half of the biscuit on the egg.
5. **Serve:**
   - Serve the breakfast biscuit sandwiches immediately while warm.

**Variations:**

- **Add vegetables:** You can add sliced tomatoes, avocado, or spinach to the sandwich for extra flavor and nutrition.
- **Sauce it up:** Add a dollop of hot sauce, ketchup, or mayonnaise to enhance the flavor.
- **Make it spicy:** Use spicy sausage or add a slice of jalapeño for a kick.

This breakfast biscuit sandwich with egg and sausage is a delicious and portable breakfast option that's perfect for busy mornings or as a weekend treat. Enjoy the combination of savory sausage, creamy egg, melted cheese, and fluffy biscuit!

**Yogurt and Berry Smoothie**

**Ingredients:**

- 1 cup plain Greek yogurt (or any yogurt of your choice)
- 1 cup mixed berries (such as strawberries, blueberries, raspberries)
- 1 ripe banana, sliced (optional, for added sweetness and creaminess)
- 1 tablespoon honey or maple syrup (optional, for additional sweetness)
- 1/2 cup milk (dairy or non-dairy, adjust quantity as needed for desired consistency)
- Ice cubes (optional, for a colder smoothie)

**Instructions:**

1. **Prepare the Ingredients:**
   - If using frozen berries, you can use them straight from the freezer. If using fresh berries, rinse them thoroughly.
2. **Blend the Ingredients:**
   - In a blender, combine the yogurt, mixed berries, sliced banana (if using), honey or maple syrup (if using), and milk.
   - If desired, add a handful of ice cubes to make the smoothie colder and thicker.
3. **Blend Until Smooth:**
   - Blend on high speed until the mixture is smooth and creamy. Stop to scrape down the sides of the blender if needed.
4. **Adjust Consistency:**
   - If the smoothie is too thick, add more milk, a little at a time, until you reach your desired consistency. If it's too thin, add more yogurt or frozen berries.
5. **Serve:**
   - Pour the smoothie into glasses and serve immediately.
   - Optionally, garnish with a few whole berries on top for presentation.

**Tips:**

- You can customize this smoothie by adding other ingredients like spinach or kale for added nutrients, a scoop of protein powder for extra protein, or a spoonful of chia seeds for fiber.
- Adjust the sweetness by adding more or less honey or maple syrup according to your taste preference.
- This smoothie can be made ahead of time and stored in the refrigerator for up to 24 hours. Give it a stir before serving.

Enjoy this creamy and fruity yogurt and berry smoothie as a refreshing and nutritious start to your day or as a quick pick-me-up any time!